TM 9-721
WAR DEPARTMENT MANUAL

M6 AND M6A1 HEAVY TANKS TECHNICAL MANUAL

BY **WAR DEPARTMENT**

DECLASSIFIED

RESTRICTED — Dissemination of restricted matter. —The information contained in restricted documents and the essential characteristics of restricted material may be given to any person known to be in the service of the United States and to persons of undoubted loyalty and discretion who are cooperating in Government work, but will not be communicated to the public or in the press except by authorized military public relations agencies. (See also par. 18b, AR 330-5, 28 Sep 1942.)

WAR DEPARTMENT · 5 FEBRUARY, 1943

©2011 PERISCOPE FILM LLC
ALL RIGHTS RESERVED
ISBN #978-1-935700-83-8
WWW.PERISCOPEFILM.COM

~~RESTRICTED~~

WAR DEPARTMENT

TECHNICAL MANUAL

DECLASSIFIED

HEAVY TANKS M6 AND M6A1

FEBRUARY 5, 1943

DECLASSIFIED

~~RESTRICTED~~

TM 9-721

TECHNICAL MANUAL
No. 9-721

WAR DEPARTMENT
Washington, February 5, 1943

HEAVY TANKS M6 AND M6A1

Prepared under the direction of the
Chief of Ordnance

CONTENTS

		Paragraphs	Pages
PART ONE — Operating Instructions			
SECTION I.	Introduction	1– 5	3– 10
II.	Operation and controls	6–13	11– 24
III.	Armament	14–16	25– 28
IV.	Preventive maintenance	17–21	29– 43
V.	Lubrication	22–27	44– 49
VI.	Care and preservation	28–29	50
VII.	Tools and equipment	30–31	51– 60
VIII.	Operation under unusual conditions	32–35	61– 63
IX.	Materiel affected by chemicals	36–39	64– 66
PART TWO — Organization Instructions			
X.	General information on maintenance	40	67– 70
XI.	Tools and equipment	41–42	71– 75
XII.	Organization spare parts and accessories	43	76
XIII.	Engine and accessories	44–49	77–100
XIV.	Fuel system	50–53	101–105
XV.	Cooling system	54–55	106
XVI.	Torque converter	56–58	107–111
XVII.	Hycon system	59–61	112–115
XVIII.	Power train	62–64	116–117

1

TM 9-721   **HEAVY TANKS M6 AND M6A1**

		Paragraphs	Pages
Section	XIX. Suspension and tracks	65–75	118–128
	XX. Electrical system	76–83	129–145
	XXI. Painting	84–89	146–148
	XXII. Shipment and storage	90–92	149–154
	XXIII. References	93–94	155–157
Index			158–168

PART ONE — Operating Instructions

Section I
INTRODUCTION

	Paragraph
Scope	1
Contents and arrangement of manual	2
Characteristics	3
Differences among models	4
Data	5

1. SCOPE.

   a. This manual is intended to serve temporarily (pending the publication of a more complete revision) to give information and guidance to the personnel of the using arms charged with the operation, maintenance and minor repairs of this materiel.

   b. Disassembly, assembly and such repairs as may be handled by the using arm personnel will be undertaken only under the supervision of an officer or the chief mechanic.

   c. In all cases where the nature of the repair, modification, or adjustment is beyond the scope or facilities of the unit, the responsible ordnance service should be informed in order that trained personnel with suitable tools and equipment may be provided, or proper instructions issued.

2. CONTENTS AND ARRANGEMENT OF MANUAL.

   a. The manual is divided into two parts. Part One consists of sections I through IX which contain information chiefly for the guidance of operating personnel. Part Two consists of sections X through XXIII, and contains information chiefly for the guidance of the using arm personnel doing maintenance work.

3. CHARACTERISTICS (figs. 1, 2, 3, 4, and 5).

   a. Heavy Tanks M6 and M6A1 are armored, full tracklaying vehicles, each powered by an aviation-type, radial, 9-cylinder, air-cooled gasoline engine.

   b. The engine is located in a compartment directly behind the driving compartment. Access to the engine, for replacement of certain accessories and the performance of limited maintenance operations, is provided by a door in the front engine compartment bulkhead, four hatch covers in the engine compartment top plate, and two removable inspection plates in the floor of the engine compartment.

   c. The assembled torque converter, transmission and final drive are mounted directly behind the engine. The driving sprockets are thus at

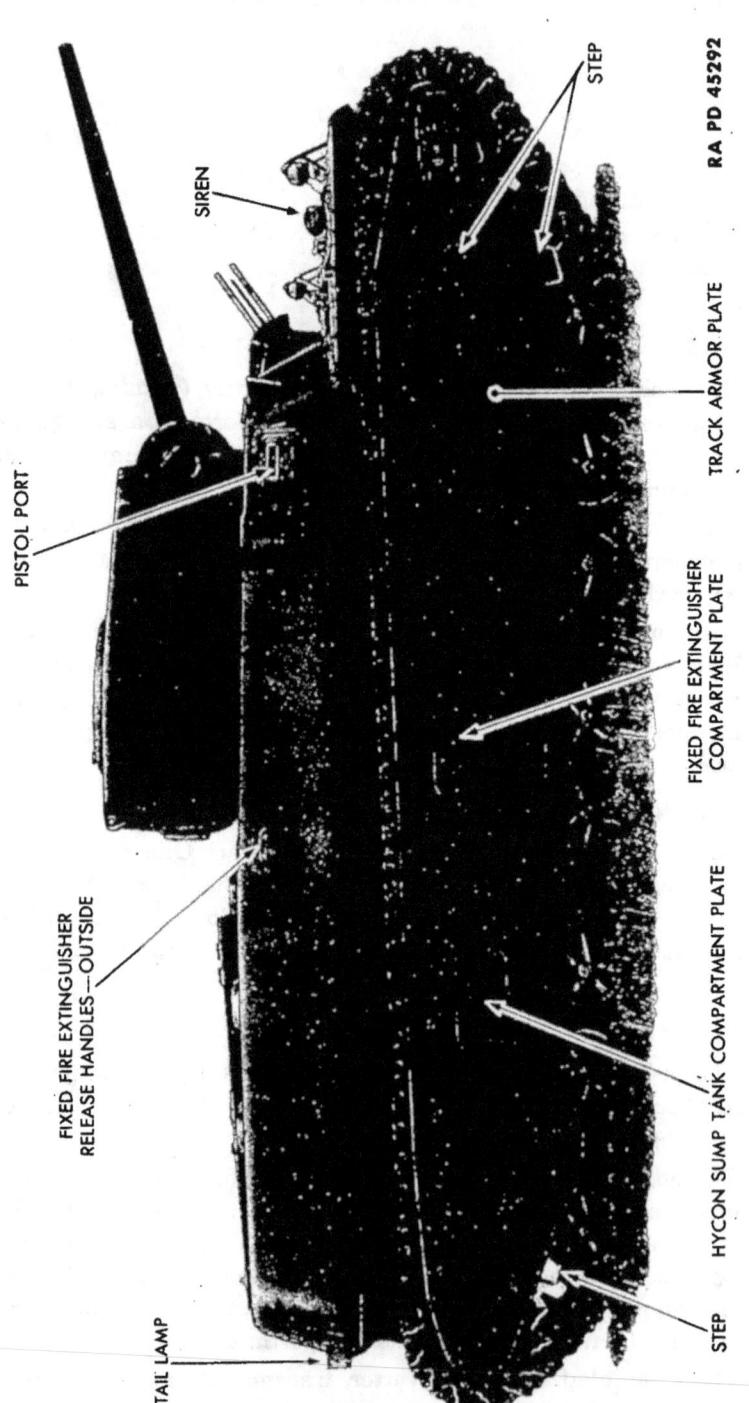

Figure 1 — Right Side View — Heavy Tank M6

INTRODUCTION

TM 9-721
3

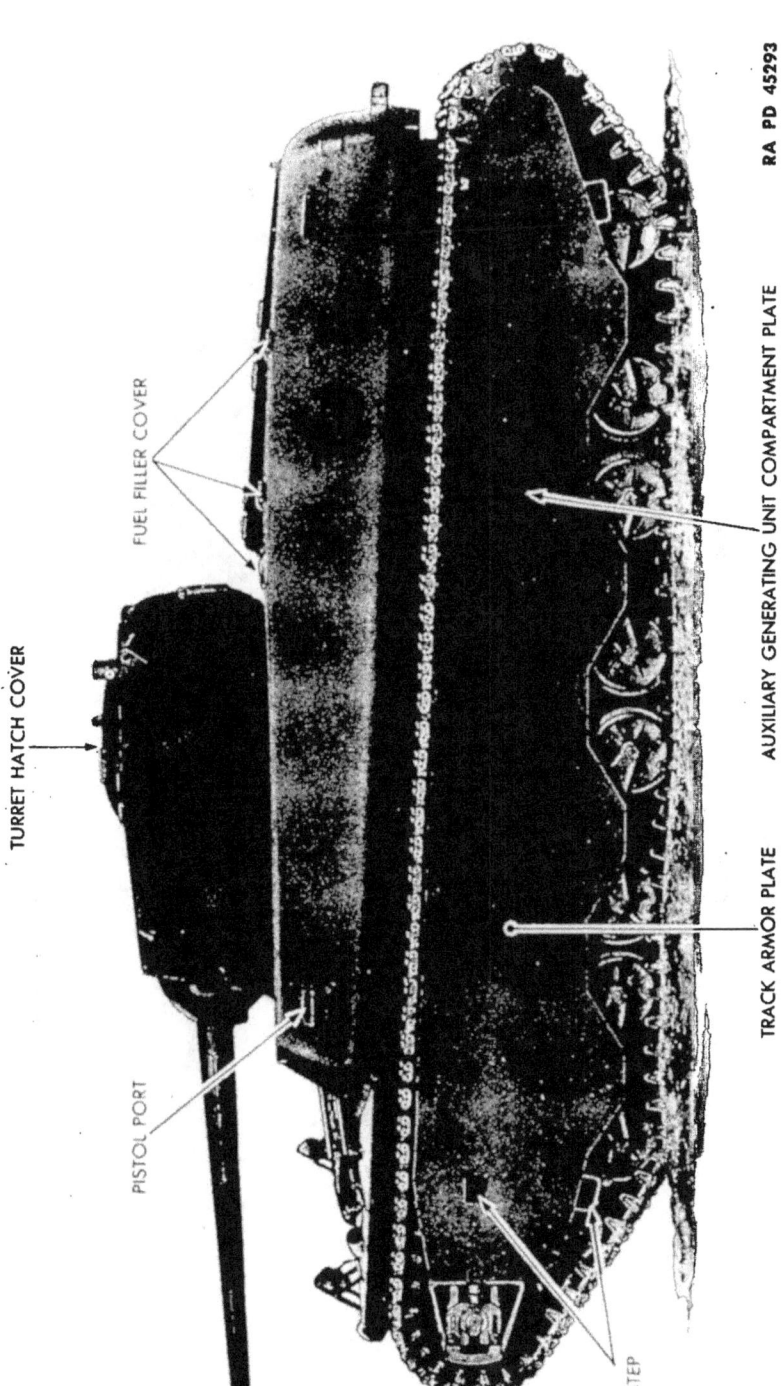

Figure 2 — Left Side View — Heavy Tank M6

Figure 3—Three-quarter Left Front View—Heavy Tank M6

INTRODUCTION

TM 9-721
3

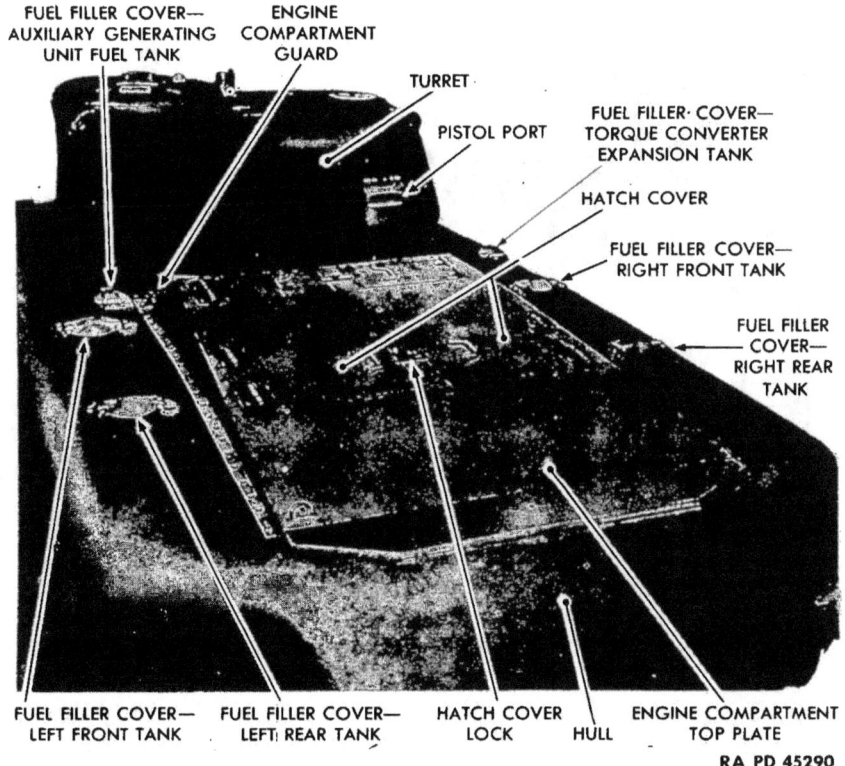

Figure 4—Top Rear View—Heavy Tank M6

the rear of the vehicle, differing from the position of the sprockets as used on the medium tanks. A flexible coupling connects the engine to the torque converter, no propeller shaft being used on this vehicle. The hydraulic torque converter is a form of hydraulic transmission which applies the engine horsepower to the final drive. Fluid, such as No. 1 grade Diesel fuel, is the operating medium of the torque converter, there being no mechanical connection between the input and output ends of the torque converter. Since the drive is through fluid, no clutch is used on the vehicle. A pedal, placed in the position usually occupied by a clutch pedal, serves as a transmission brake pedal. In order to shift, the converter turbine and transmission gears must be slowed down or stopped by means of the brake. Two forward speeds and one reverse speed are provided.

d. Tracks used on the Heavy Tanks M6 and M6A1 are double tracks, a track block consisting of 2 shoes held together by connecting pins. Pins are bare between the shoes, to provide space for a center track connector. This differs from the conventional track connector in that it

HEAVY TANKS M6 AND M6A1

Figure 5—Top Rear View with Hatch Doors Open—Heavy Tank M6

consists of two parts which clamp around the pins, held together by a bolt and safety type nut. Track shoes are half rubber and half steel, the rubber section being placed on the inside of the track to run next to the bogie wheels and idlers when the track is installed. Tracks may not be reversed, although under certain conditions, and when approved by the officer in charge of maintenance, they may be turned end for end.

e. A main idler is provided to adjust each track. Idlers are designed to slide forward and back in two slots in the idler block, adjustment being provided by drilled jackscrews. An auxiliary, nonadjustable idler is mounted between the main idler and the front bogie assembly. Under ordinary traveling conditions on level terrain, the track does not ride against the auxiliary idler. When crossing rough terrain, the auxiliary idler acts to provide additional track support between the main idler and front bogie assembly.

f. Each bogie assembly has 4 bogie wheels. Two shafts, on each of which are mounted 2 of the bogie wheels, are clamped together at each end and in the center. Two volute springs are mounted horizontally between the 2 shafts and wheels.

g. The armor of the hull front section is $3\frac{5}{8}$ inches thick; the armor on the sides is $2\frac{1}{16}$ inches thick in front of the bulkhead, and $1\frac{5}{8}$ inches thick in back of the bulkhead; the roof is 1 inch thick; the rear section is $1\frac{13}{16}$ inches thick, and the floor plate is 1 inch thick.

INTRODUCTION   **TM 9-721**
                       3-5

    h. The armor of the turret at the front is 1¾ inches thick, at the sides and rear 3¼ inches thick, and on the roof 1 inch thick.

    i. An auxiliary electrical generating system, consisting of a generating set powered by a single cylinder gasoline engine, is mounted in the left rear sponson. This unit is used to charge the batteries.

4. DIFFERENCES AMONG MODELS.

    a. In all characteristics of design and equipment affecting operation, care, and maintenance, Heavy Tanks M6 and M6A1 are identical. The only difference is in the hull construction: Heavy Tank M6 is of cast hull construction, and Heavy Tank M6A1 is of welded hull construction. At the time of preparation of this manual, no figure was available to show the welded hull construction, only the cast hull being shown. However, in construction, the welded hull is quite similar to the hull construction used in the Medium Tank M4.

5. DATA.

    a. General.

Over-all length (approximate) .... 23 ft 10 in.
Over-all height (approximate) .... 9 ft 10 in.
Over-all width (approximate) .... 10 ft 3 in.

    b. Engine.

Make .... Wright Aeronautical Corporation
Type .... Static, radial, air-cooled
Number of cylinders .... 9, single row
Rated horsepower and revolutions per minute .... 800 at 2,300 rpm
Weight (including governor, oil pump, oil filter, fuel pump, fuel
    primer, carburetor, generator, spark plugs, ignition shielding,
    magnetos, starting motor) .... 1,350 lb

    c. Armament.

GUN, 3-in., M7 (T-49 combination mount), in turret (1)
GUN, 37-mm (T-49 combination mount), in turret (1)
GUN, machine, cal. .30, M1919A4 (flexible), on turret hatch cover (1)
GUN, machine, cal. .30, M1919A4, in bow of hull (1)
GUN, machine, cal. .50, M2, HB (twin mount T-52), in bow of hull (2)
GUN, Thompson, submachine, cal. .45, M1928A1, one in front right-hand
    sponson and one in turret (2)

    d. Ammunition Carried.

3-in. ammunition .... 75 rounds
37-mm ammunition .... 202 rounds
Cal. .30 ammunition .... 5,500 rounds
Cal. .50 ammunition .... 6,900 rounds
Cal. .45 ammunition .... 1,200 rounds
Hand grenades 24

9

HEAVY TANKS M6 AND M6A1

e. **Communication.**
Radio set .... SCR 506, sending and receiving
Intra-tank .... Telephone

f. **Fuel Tanks.**
Type .... Fabric and synthetic rubber
Number of fuel tanks 4
Total capacity .... 477 gal

Section II

OPERATION AND CONTROLS

	Paragraph
General	6
Controls	7
Prestarting inspection	8
Engine starting and warm-up	9
Inspections during engine warm-up	10
Operating vehicle	11
Stopping the engine	12
Operating precautions	13

6. GENERAL.

a. Due to the fact there is no mechanical connection between the engine and tracks, the *feel* and operation of the Heavy Tanks M6 and M6A1 are somewhat different from the lighter, conventional, medium tanks. In addition, there is a minimum of shifting, no clutching, and completely hydraulic steering lever operation. For these reasons the competent medium tank driver should not feel qualified to drive the Heavy Tanks M6 and M6A1 without first familiarizing himself fully with the controls of the vehicle.

7. CONTROLS.

a. **Position of Driver.** The driver sits on the left side of the front compartment, directly behind the Hycon control pedestal (fig. 6).

b. **Steering Controls** (fig. 6).

(1) HYCON.

(a) Two Hycon steering controls, about 4 inches high, project upward through slots in the control box on the Hycon pedestal. These are used to steer the vehicle under all normal driving conditions. To steer the vehicle, pull back the control on the side toward which it is desired to turn. Little effort is needed to move the controls and only short travel distance is necessary to place the hydraulic system in effect. Pulling back either one of the controls slows down the track on that side, while the speed of the other track is increased. Thus the vehicle turns with power on both tracks at all times.

(b) The button in the top of each of the 2 Hycon controls fires the cal. .30 machine gun in the bow of the vehicle. The gun safety switches on the instrument panel must be switched on (fig. 7) and the buttons in the 2 controls must be pressed simultaneously in order to fire the gun.

Figure 6 — Driving Controls

OPERATION AND CONTROLS

(c) Stop light switches, actuated by the operation of the controls, are incorporated within the control box. Stop lights flash on when both controls are pulled back together.

(2) MANUAL.

(a) Two steering levers provided with rubber grips are mounted directly in front of the driver, one on each side of the pedestal control box. These are similar in appearance and operation to the conventional-type steering levers used on the medium tanks. *They are used for steering purposes, however, only when the hydraulic Hycon controls are inoperative.*

(b) A ratchet is installed at the base of each steering lever. When the handles in the top of the steering levers are rotated one-quarter turn, the steering levers may be locked at any desired position along the ratchet. Steering levers are pulled back simultaneously, and locked in the full rear position, to provide parking brakes for the vehicle.

(c) Connected to the top (front) of each manual steering lever is a gun firing control lever. In the event that the Hycon controls are rendered inoperative, necessitating the use of the manual steering levers, the cal. .30 machine gun in the bow of the vehicle may be fired by pulling back on both of the gun firing control levers simultaneously. The gun safety switches on the instrument panel must be on.

(d) Stop light switches, actuated by the operation of the steering levers, are installed at the base of each lever. Stop lights flash on when both steering levers are pulled back together.

c. Accelerator and Hand Throttle (fig. 6). A foot accelerator pedal is located on the floor to the right of the manual steering levers. A hand-operated throttle is also provided.

d. Brakes.

(1) SERVICE BRAKES. Pulling back simultaneously on both Hycon controls slows down or stops the driving sprockets, depending on the effort applied, and thus slows or stops the vehicle.

(2) PARKING BRAKES. Manual steering levers are used as parking brakes on the Heavy Tanks M6 and M6A1. A detailed discussion of the use of the steering levers as parking brakes is given above (par. 7 b (2)).

(3) TRANSMISSION BRAKE. The transmission brake pedal (fig. 6) is located to the left of the manual steering levers, convenient to the driver's left foot. To permit shifting of the gears, the converter turbine and transmission gears must first be brought to a full stop. Stepping on the transmission brake pedal operates brake shoes against the transmission brake disk, slowing down or stopping transmission gears in direct proportion to the effort applied.

e. **Siren Control.** The foot-operated siren button is located in the footrest beneath the transmission brake pedal (fig. 6), within easy reach of the driver's left foot.

f. **Clutch.** No clutch is provided on the vehicle.

g. **Gear Shifting.**

(1) Shifting of gears in the transmission for speed changes is accomplished by two gearshift hand levers, located on the hull to the left of the driver (fig. 6).

(2) The lever nearest the front of the vehicle is the gearshift lever. It has three positions. The forward position is low speed, center position is neutral, and the back position is high speed. The second lever on the hull is the selector gearshift lever. It has two positions, forward and back. *While driving in either of the two forward speeds, the selector gearshift lever must always be in the forward position.* To shift into reverse gear, release the accelerator pedal and drop engine revolutions to below 800 revolutions per minute. Step on the transmission brake pedal and bring transmission gears to a full stop. Shift the gearshift lever into neutral. Pull the selector gearshift lever to its rear position, then pull the gearshift lever back into what was the high-speed position. This will now be reverse speed.

h. **Cal. .30 Bow Machine Gun Elevation Control Lever.** Mounted on a cross shaft across the front of the hull, and projecting out along the side of the hull to the left of the driver is the cal. .30 bow machine gun elevation control lever (fig. 6). The lever is equipped with a latch button which locks the gun at any desired elevation within its elevating range.

i. **Primer Pump.** Mounted on a bracket extending down from the hull, directly in front of the driver, is the engine primer pump (fig. 6).

j. **Instrument Panel** (fig. 7). The instrument panel is located at eye level to the left of the driver on the sponson wall. It carries the speedometer, tachometer, Hycon pressure gage, ignition and starter switches, gun safety switch, oil dilution switch, light switches, cylinder temperature gage, gas gage selector, engine oil temperature and oil pressure gages, torque converter oil temperature and oil pressure gages, voltmeter, ammeter, final drive oil temperature and oil pressure gages, clock, and sockets for the windshield wiper, defrosters and trouble light.

k. **Compass.** The compass is mounted in brackets on the hull, in front and to the left of the driver.

l. **Oil Pressure Warning Light.**

(1) Mounted on the bracket which also holds the compass to the front of the hull is an oil pressure warning light. The light flashes red

OPERATION AND CONTROLS

TM 9-721
7

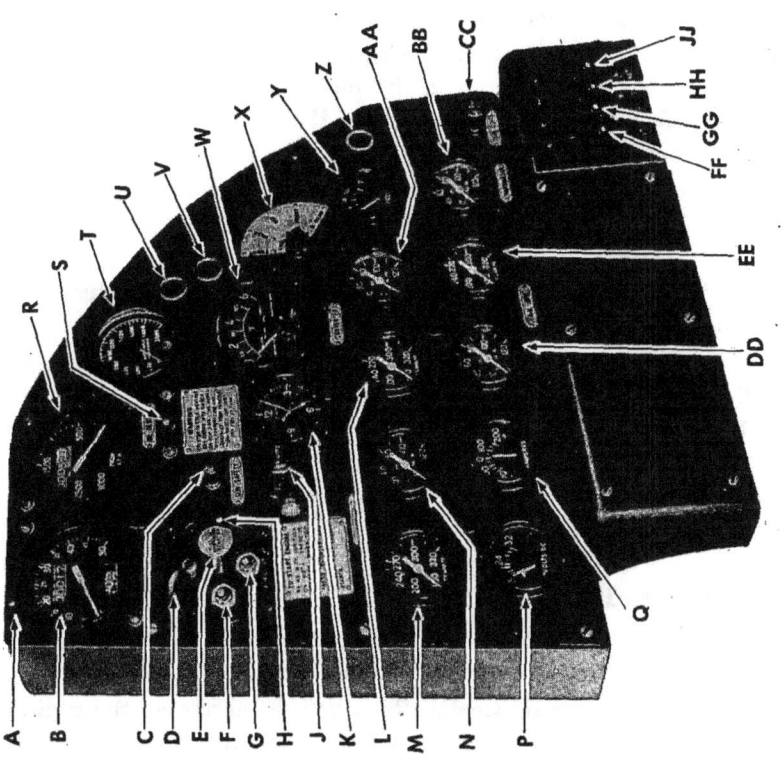

Figure 7 — Instrument Panel

A — SPEEDOMETER RESET
B — SPEEDOMETER
C — GUN SAFETY SWITCH
D — MAGNETO SWITCH
E — ENERGIZED STARTER SWITCH
F — BOOSTER SWITCH
G — FUEL CUT-OFF SWITCH
H — STARTER SWITCH
J — HEADLIGHT SWITCH
K — CLOCK
L — CONVERTER OIL TEMPERATURE GAGE
M — ENGINE OIL TEMPERATURE GAGE
N — ENGINE OIL PRESSURE GAGE
P — VOLTMETER
Q — AMMETER
R — TACHOMETER
S — OIL DILUTION SWITCH
T — HYCON PRESSURE GAGE
U — WINDSHIELD WIPER SOCKET
V — TROUBLE LIGHT SOCKET
W — CYLINDER TEMPERATURE GAGE
X — FUEL GAGE SELECTOR
Y — FUEL GAGE
Z — DEFROSTER SOCKET
AA — CONVERTER OIL PRESSURE GAGE
BB — TRANSMISSION OIL PRESSURE GAGE
CC — PANEL LIGHT SWITCH
DD — FINAL DRIVE OIL PRESSURE GAGE
EE — FINAL DRIVE OIL TEMPERATURE GAGE
FF — MAIN LIGHT SWITCH
GG — MAIN ENGINE ELECTRICAL SWITCH (COIL)
HH — BOW CAL. .30 MACHINE GUN MAIN FIRING SWITCH
JJ — MAIN BATTERY SWITCH

RA PD 45273

15

when oil pressure drops below 25 pounds. If, when operating the vehicle with engine at normal operating temperature, the light flashes on, stop the engine immediately and investigate the cause or report to the responsible ordnance maintenance personnel.

CAUTION: When starting a cold engine, it will naturally take a few seconds for oil to reach operating pressure. During this time the red warning light will flash on and remain on until proper oil pressure is obtained. Do not interpret the flashing of the warning light at this time as indicating an inoperative oil pump or other malfunction.

  m. **Fire Detector Light** (fig. 6). Mounted on the Hycon control box, directly in front of the driver, is the fire detector light. Seven fire detectors, spaced about the engine compartment, are connected to the fire detector light. In the event of fire in the engine compartment, causing the flame to touch one of the fire detectors, the detector automatically grounds the circuit, lighting the red fire detector light.

  n. **Fire Extinguisher Handles.** Two fire extinguisher handles are mounted inside the driving compartment on the right side of the hull directly behind the mount for the bow cal. .30 machine gun (fig. 13). Two fire extinguisher handles are also mounted outside the vehicle on the right center side of the hull (fig. 14).

  o. **Fuel Shut-off Valve Handles** (figs. 24 and 25). Five fuel shut-off valve handles are provided, one for each of the four tanks, and one main shut-off valve handle. Shut-off valve handles for the left and right tanks project out into the left and right rear of the driving compartment. The main shut-off valve handle is mounted in the left center of the front engine compartment bulkhead.

8. PRESTARTING INSPECTION.

  a. **General.** Before the engine is started or the vehicle put into operation, a careful and complete inspection should be made.

  b. **Check for Oil and Fuel Leaks.** Remove the guard over the engine compartment, and open the engine and transmission compartment hatch covers (figs. 4 and 5). Note any unusual presence of gasoline fumes, or evidence of leaking fuel or oil lines, as shown by oil or fuel on the floor of the engine compartment or around the carburetor or fuel and oil pumps. Failure to keep lines and fittings tight and in good condition can cause a major failure.

  c. **Turn Handles of Oil Filters.** Turn the cleaning handles of the converter oil filters one complete turn to the right. This cleans the dirt from the edges of the filters. Failure to turn the handles a complete turn each day will allow filters to clog and permit oil to bypass directly into the converter or reduction gearing.

OPERATION AND CONTROLS

d. Check Reduction Gear Oil Level. Remove combination breather cap and oil level gage from reduction gear case to check reduction gear oil level. No additional oil should be needed between periodic changes. However, should oil have to be added frequently between periodic changes, check for source and cause of leak, and repair or report to proper authority.

e. Check Operating Fluid Level in Expansion Tank. Remove breather-filter cap from expansion tank. Level gage indicator (bayonet-type) must indicate that some fluid is in the reserve tank. Final check and addition of fluid should be made during engine warm-up.

f. Change Oil in Air Cleaners. Unless the vehicle has been operating in wet weather, snow, or under unusually dust-free conditions, the oil in the air cleaners should be changed daily. Under dusty conditions it may be necessary to service the air cleaners even more frequently. To change the oil, remove the oil reservoir from the bottom of the air cleaner, then remove the lower filter section. Pour out the oil from the oil reservoir, and scrape out the dirt. Clean the lower filter section with SOLVENT, dry-cleaning, and install it in place on the filter. Fill the oil reservoir up to the oil line indicated on the reservoir, using OIL, lubricating, engine, SAE 30, above 32 F, and OIL, lubricating, engine, SAE 10, below 32 F. Install the oil reservoir.

g. Clean Carburetor Screen. Remove carburetor screen. Wash screen with SOLVENT, dry-cleaning, being sure that all trace of dirt is removed. Install screen, being careful to tighten it just tight enough to prevent leaks. Excessive tightening will spread or otherwise injure the lead gasket.

h. Clean Oil Pump Finger Strainer. It is not necessary to clean the oil pump finger strainer daily, but it must be cleaned after every 15 hours of operation. Remove the oil pump finger strainer. Wash strainer in SOLVENT, dry-cleaning. Clean the spring and retaining nut. Install strainer, insert spring, install copper gaskets, and screw retainer nut in place.

i. Check for Oil or Fuel in the Lower Cylinders. Rotate the engine crankshaft by energizing the starter for a few seconds; then open and close the starter engagement switch. Continue this operation through three or more complete revolutions. If no unusual resistance is encountered during the first three revolutions, continue to turn the crankshaft through several more revolutions, without stopping, to insure complete freedom of rotation. If any unusual resistance is indicated, remove one spark plug from each of the lower cylinders to allow any fuel or oil to drain out. Rotate the engine several times. CAUTION: Operating the starter continuously without previously checking the engine as outlined above may cause serious damage to the internal parts of the engine if oil or fuel has drained into the combustion chambers.

j. Check Instrument Panel (fig. 7).

(1) Inspect the voltmeter (switch open) to see that the needle is against the stop.

(2) Close battery switch and check voltmeter for 24-volt reading, and check ammeter for zero reading.

(3) Check fuel gage, switching the selector to all four tanks, for adequate fuel supply.

(4) Check headlight and siren operation, watching ammeter for indication of discharge.

(5) Check operation of solenoid fuel cut-off switch.

k. Other Inspections Before Starting.

(1) Check the accelerator pedal for free operation without binding.

(2) Check hand throttle operation for freedom of movement.

(3) Check gearshift lever and selector gearshift lever operation, making sure levers can be shifted into all operating positions.

(4) Check action of manual steering levers as parking brakes by pulling both levers back to a full rear position, locking them, then unlocking them and returning to their forward position.

(5) Check engine oil level and transmission oil level.

(6) Check equipment.

(7) Inspect sprockets, bogies, track support rollers and idlers.

(8) Check tracks for wear and tension.

(9) Check to see that field equipment and rations are correctly loaded.

9. ENGINE STARTING AND WARM-UP.

a. Easy starting, operating efficiency, and the effective life of the engine are greatly influenced by the care used by the driver in starting and warming up the engine. For these reasons it is essential that the following procedure be followed every time the engine is started, even though the vehicle is to be moved only a short distance.

b. Procedure.

(1) Have engine turned over 4 complete crankshaft revolutions by hand (about 50 turns of the hand crank).

(2) Open fuel shut-off valves (figs. 24 and 25).

(3) Switch on the main battery switch, engine electrical switch and light switch (fig. 7).

(4) Turn on the booster switch and listen for the buzzing sound which indicates operation (fig. 7).

(5) See that gearshift lever and selector gearshift lever are in neutral position (fig. 6).

OPERATION AND CONTROLS

(6) Unless the engine is already warmed up, prime the engine 5 strokes of the primer pump (pull plunger out slowly, push in briskly) (fig. 6). Avoid overpriming, which tends to wash the oil off cylinder walls.

(7) Open the hand throttle slightly.

(8) Pull out the energized starter switch, and wind the starting motor for 3 or 4 seconds (fig. 7).

(9) Close the starter and booster switches (fig. 7). (If necessary, continue to prime the engine while starting.) CAUTION: Never hold the starter switch closed for more than 30 seconds at a time. Then allow starting motor to cool off before attempting to turn the engine over again.

(10) Wait 2 seconds, then turn the magneto switch to the "BOTH" position (fig. 7). If the engine fails to start, repeat the process. After engine starts, press lightly on accelerator pedal (fig. 6). *Do not pump throttle.* Too much gas when the engine first starts will cause it to stall. NOTE: If the engine has been overprimed, and is flooded, turn it over with the starting motor, holding the accelerator wide open, with the ignition switch on.

(11) Continue to prime until the engine is firing smoothly and the fuel pressure builds up to its running limit of 15 to 18 pounds per square inch. If the engine is warm, priming may not be necessary.

(12) As soon as the engine starts, *watch the engine and converter oil pressure gages* (fig. 7). If oil does not start building up pressure on the gages within 10 seconds, at 800 revolutions per minute, shut off the engine and report the condition to the proper authorities.

(13) Warm the engine at *800 revolutions per minute for 5 minutes.* The engine oil pressure should be between 55 and 75 pounds, which is normal for this engine speed. Converter oil pressure gage should read between 35 and 45 pounds.

(14) After a 5 minute period, and if engine and converter oil temperatures have reached 100 F, increase engine speed to 1,000 revolutions per minute. If oil pressure drops off, go back to 800 revolutions per minute for more complete warm-up.

(15) Check operation of instruments while warming up, and note results on commander's report. The ammeter reading immediately after starting may be as high as 55 amperes, depending upon the condition of the batteries, and will gradually drop as the batteries become charged. The voltmeter, after starting, may be as high as 28½ volts (fig. 7).

(16) Increase engine speed to 1,800 revolutions per minute and check fuel pressure and engine operation with magneto switch in "L" and "R" positions (fig. 7). A 200 revolution-per-minute drop in engine speed is permissible at this speed, when operating on only 1 magneto and using

80 octane fuel. CAUTION: Do not run engine on 1 magneto for more than a 30-second interval, as this will cause the inoperative plugs to become carbonized.

(17) CHECK CONVERTER OIL LEVEL. Check fluid level in expansion tank for proper operating level. Should expansion tank level gage indicate no fluid in expansion tank, add proper quantity, and fluid pressure gage will indicate proper operating pressure.

(18) CLEAN CONVERTER ORIFICE VENT VALVE (fig. 10). Clean orifice vent valve by turning handle from operating position to clean position (90° turn to stop) and return immediately to operating position when fluid sprays out. This must be done while engine is running and fluid circulating in system. Failure to clean orifice vent valve daily will cause it to clog up, trapping air or gas in converter fluid circuit, which in turn lowers the efficiency of the converter, causing excessive heating and loss of power.

(19) PRECAUTIONS IN ENGINE OPERATION.

(a) Never idle below 800 revolutions per minute at any time, and never idle at 800 revolutions per minute for more than 5 minutes. Preferable idling speed is 1,000 revolutions per minute. Continuous idling will appreciably shorten the useful life of the engine.

(b) Normal oil pressure should never be below 55 pounds, and should be 65 to 75 pounds at operating speed of 2,300 revolutions per minute.

(c) Never lug engine below 1,600 revolutions per minute.

(d) Engine oil temperature should be 160 to 180 F at operating speeds.

(e) Operate engine from 2,000 to 2,300 revolutions per minute. Minimum operating speeds for brief periods only, 1,700 to 1,900 revolutions per minute.

(f) Since the Heavy Tanks M6 and M6A1 are equipped with a hydraulic torque converter, eliminating any mechanical connection between the engine and tracks, it is impossible to start the engine by towing or coasting.

(g) Care must be taken not to allow dirt to collect on cylinders, nor to permit any object to block the flow of air to or from the cylinders, as this may cause overheating and preignition.

10. INSPECTIONS DURING ENGINE WARM-UP.

a. The following inspections are to be made before and during the time required for engine warm-up.

b. **Procédure.**

(1) INSPECT FOR OIL LEAKS UNDER THE HULL. This inspection is made from both the front and the rear, and is one of the first inspections

OPERATION AND CONTROLS

made or ordered by the commander. Trace possible cause of any leaks, and correct the condition.

(2) INSPECT TRACK FOR TENSION. If the track shows noticeable sag, it must be tightened (par. 71).

(3) INSPECT CONDITION OF TRACK. Check connectors for worn, bent or broken guide lugs. Inspect all wedges and nuts for presence and tightness. Check presence of self-locking nuts. Check for bottomed wedges, and replace. Inspect all slack portions of the track for the presence of dead track blocks and replace any such blocks. The presence of a dead track block is indicated by a block which has dropped definitely out of line. NOTE: To be detected, a dead track block must be on the top of the track. This necessitates moving the vehicle to make a complete inspection. At this time the inside wedges and connectors can also be inspected.

(4) INSPECT SPROCKETS. Check for sprung or worn teeth. Check cap screws and hub nuts for tightness. Check inside cap screws when vehicle is being moved.

(5) INSPECT BOGIE WHEELS. Check condition of tires on all wheels. Look for evidence of outer spacer turning, and tighten gudgeon nut if spacer is turning. Check presence of gudgeon nuts, and see that cotter pins are properly installed. Check condition of grease fittings and release valves, and replace any that are damaged or missing.

(6) INSPECT BOGIE ASSEMBLIES. Check for broken or weak volute springs. Inspect wheel arm and lever wear plates for wear, and replace if worn. Inspect bogie brackets for presence of bolts, nuts and lock wire.

(7) INSPECT SUPPORT ROLLERS. Look for evidence of roller not turning, and free up all rollers by cleaning out mud, rocks, etc. Check grease fittings, and replace missing fittings. It is essential that all rollers turn freely since inoperative rollers will develop flat spots.

(8) INSPECT IDLERS. Check for security of idler cap and grease fittings.

CAUTION: It is highly important that the entire track and suspension system be kept as clean as possible and free from dirt, rocks and sticks. This will protect the life and efficiency of the system.

11. OPERATING VEHICLE (figs. 6 and 7).

a. With the driver in the driver's seat, the engine at idling speed, and all instruments showing normal readings, the driver is then ready to drive the vehicle.

b. Depress transmission brake pedal, then release manual steering levers from their full rear parking brake position to a full front position.

c. Make sure selector gearshift lever is in the forward position, then shift gearshift lever into low speed.

d. After speeding up engine, gradually release transmission brake pedal, at the same time depressing the foot throttle. When a reasonable speed has been reached, according to terrain, lift the foot from the accelerator and apply the transmission brake pedal to slow down the torque converter, then pull the gearshift lever back to the high-speed position. Release the transmission brake pedal and depress the accelerator pedal to resume speed.

e. Correct gear for running is that which enables the vehicle to proceed at the desired speed without causing the engine to labor. Do not ride the transmission brake pedal. The driver's left foot must be completely removed from transmission brake pedal while driving to avoid unnecessary wear of the transmission brake shoes.

f. To place vehicle in reverse, a complete stop must be made, and throttle closed to idling speed. Step on the transmission brake to stop the converter turbine and transmission gears. Pull the selector gearshift lever to the rear position, then shift the gearshift lever back into what was the high-speed position. The vehicle will now be in reverse speed. Do not back up vehicle unless an observer is stationed in front to guide the driver.

g. To steer, pull back the right-hand Hycon control to make a right turn, and the left-hand control to make a left turn. This action keeps one of the tracks from turning as fast as the other, thus more power is needed. As the driver anticipates making a turn, he must be ready to apply the foot throttle to a greater extent, depending on the sharpness of the turn.

h. To stop the vehicle, release the throttle and pull back on both Hycon controls simultaneously, depressing transmission brake pedal when the vehicle has slowed down to approximately 2 to 5 miles per hour, depending on which gear is being employed before stopping. It is desirable to shift into the low speed before stopping, and use engine drag to slow the vehicle, to facilitate stopping.

i. The manual steering levers, when locked in the full rear position, serve as the parking brake. Use the manual steering levers only for parking, never for steering the vehicle except in cases of emergency when the Hycon controls are rendered inoperative. Always make sure the manual steering levers are released from their full rear position before putting the vehicle in motion.

j. Tachometer, oil temperature and oil pressure gages give the most satisfactory indication of the engine's performance. If any of these appear to be irregular, stop the engine and investigate the cause.

12. STOPPING THE ENGINE (fig. 6).

a. Close the throttle until the engine is idling at 800 to 900 revolutions per minute.

b. Continue to run at this speed until the cylinder temperature drops to about 250 F or until as low a temperature as possible is obtained. Increase the engine speed to 1,200 revolutions per minute and run at this speed for about 30 seconds to insure optimum scavenging of the oil. Holding the throttle in this position, move the fuel cut-off switch to the "ON" position and hold it in the "ON" position until the engine stops firing.

c. Move the magneto switch to the "OFF" position after the engine has stopped. Never switch off the magnetos to stop the engine, since the engine may continue to run, due to preignition.

d. In cold weather, when a temperature of less than 23 F is expected to prevail at the start, the oil dilution system should be used. When the oil-in temperature has cooled to 100 F, restart and run the engine at approximately 1,000 revolutions per minute. Open the oil dilution valve from 1 to 4 minutes as determined by the instructions on the instrument panel (or from experience), then stop the engine as described above.

e. Shut off the main fuel supply valve.

f. Switch the main battery switch to the "OFF" position.

g. Check the converter fluid pressure. Pressure should fall to zero the instant the engine stops, provided the system is full of fluid. A lagging pressure which returns slowly to zero indicates air or gas in the fluid system. Vent system, making certain expansion tank has the proper quantity of reserve fluid.

13. OPERATING PRECAUTIONS.

a. **General Instructions.** Do not allow an untrained driver to operate the vehicle, except with personal help and supervision from a competent instructor. Operation requires definite techniques which can be learned correctly only by instruction and practice. In this manner, the maximum performance will be secured from both vehicle and engine.

b. **Precautions in Driving.**

(1) Know the vehicle, its capabilities and limitations. Learn to judge engine speed by sound. Listen for unusual noises in engine and transmission, as well as in the rest of the power train.

(2) Keep engine speeds up to 2,000 to 2,300 revolutions per minute. Never run engine at wide open throttle below 1,800 revolutions per minute.

TM 9-721
13   HEAVY TANKS M6 AND M6A1

(3) Know approximate speeds in both high and low gears, and corresponding revolutions per minute of engine. This will aid in shifting and permit driver to keep vehicle under control at all times. Standing, starting and approximately 95 percent of all maneuvering can be done in high gear.

(4) Always keep power on tracks when turning. Shift to low speed if necessary to keep engine speed up.

(5) Always get into the correct gear before attempting hills, muddy areas, or long pulls. Once vehicle has entered difficult terrain, it is too late to shift down into low speed.

(6) Turning while climbing a hill can be accomplished without lugging the engine down.

(7) Use engine as a brake when going down hills.

(8) Use engine to slow down vehicle by shifting to low speed and let the engine brake the speed. This saves wear on brakes.

(9) Remove hands from Hycon controls when not actually turning the vehicle. *Riding* the controls wears the brakes.

(10) Keep left foot on footrest and off transmission brake pedal except when actually shifting gears. *Riding* the transmission brake pedal wears the transmission brake.

(11) In moving around buildings, shops or confined spaces, use low or reverse gear. Vehicle acceleration is extremely rapid with the torque converter. It is better to let engine idle down and move slowly than to have the engine speed too high. In confined spaces, have trained guide outside vehicle to direct movement with hand signals.

(12) Learn how to cross obstacles correctly. In crossing ditches let vehicle settle gently, then give engine full power as soon as bottom is reached.

(13) In breaking over an obstacle, let vehicle rise and settle down over obstacle instead of applying full power in surmounting the obstacle.

(14) Except when necessary, never drive a vehicle that needs adjustment. It is far safer and cheaper to take a few minutes to correct faults.

(15) Constantly watch oil pressure, oil temperature and tachometer gages.

(16) Never hold engine at wide-open throttle for more than a few seconds at a time. This is an emergency speed, not a driving speed.

(17) Always set manual steering levers in parking brake position after stopping vehicle.

(18) After stopping engine, always inspect engine and vehicle (par. 19). Then fill in trip ticket.

Section III

ARMAMENT

	Paragraph
Guns and gun mounts	14
Vision devices	15
Ammunition stowage	16

14. GUNS AND GUN MOUNTS.

a. General. For detailed instruction on operation, care and preservation of gun and mounts, see pertinent technical manuals listed in section XXIII.

b. Combination Mount T-49 (fig. 3).

(1) This gun mount, located in the turret, mounts a 3-inch Gun M7 and a 37-mm Gun M6, both of which move together as a unit. The guns and mounts are so designed as to provide protection to the tank personnel under all conditions of traverse and elevation.

(2) Traverse of the two guns is secured by turning the entire turret, either by means of the electric traversing mechanism or by hand. When traversing the turret the full 360 degrees, there are three danger points which must be carefully watched. These are the right and left rear corners of the hull, and the area above and to the right and left of the twin cal. .50 machine guns mounted in the bow of the vehicle. When the 3-inch gun is fully depressed, and in position above either the right or left rear corners of the vehicle, *it must not be fired or the projectile will strike the vehicle.* When the 3-inch gun is depressed, and is traversing above the twin cal. .50 machine guns in the bow, it will strike them if they are elevated. It is the responsibility of the bow gunner to depress the machine guns when the 3-inch gun is traversing in this area. To assist the commander and warn him of these danger points, a warning gage is mounted in the turret. This gage is in the shape of the vehicle, with a pointer in the shape of the 3-inch gun. When the turret is traversed, the pointer moves in the gage, showing the position of the gun at all times. Red warning lines in the silhouette of the vehicle on the gage, indicate the dangerous traversing areas.

(3) Elevation or depression of the gun mount is accomplished by an elevating handwheel. Position of the gun mount, while the vehicle is in motion, is maintained by means of a stabilizer. The stabilizer keeps the gun sufficiently close to a fixed elevation to permit the gunner to accurately aim the gun while the vehicle is in motion over uneven terrain.

(4) Periscope M8 with Telescope M15, and Periscope M6 are used for sighting the 3-inch and 37-mm guns.

(5) Both the 37-mm gun and the 3-inch gun may be fired electrically or manually.

c. **Antiaircraft Gun Mount** (fig. 2). The antiaircraft gun mount, located on the turret hatch outside the turret, mounts a cal. .30 Machine Gun M1919A4 for antiaircraft fire. The mount permits the gun and cradle to be traversed 360 degrees right and left, by hand, when the turret hatch is open. The mount can be locked in a raised or lowered position by means of a lock and latch. The gun can be used only when the turret hatch is open and is hand-fired by a conventional firing trigger.

d. **Twin Mount T-52** (fig. 3).

(1) Two cal. .50 Machine Guns M2, HB, are mounted in the Twin Mount T-52 in the bow of the vehicle. A sight is mounted between the two guns, and moves with them through all ranges of elevation and depression. The guns are elevated, traversed and fired by hand.

(2) A red warning light is mounted in the rotor of the mount. As previously explained (b (2) above), if the cal. .50 machine guns are elevated when the 3-inch gun is depressed and is traversing above them, the 3-inch gun will strike the machine guns. To warn the bow gunner of the approach of the 3-inch gun in traverse, electrical devices, actuated by the traverse of the turret in the dangerous area, switch on the red flashing light in the rotor of the twin cal. .50 machine gun mount. It is the responsibility of the bow gunner to depress the machine guns and permit the traverse of the 3-inch gun.

e. **Bow Cal. .30 Machine Gun** (figs. 3, 4 and 13).

(1) Mounted in the extreme right of the bow of the vehicle is a cal. .30 machine gun. No traverse is provided, the gun being aimed by the position of the vehicle. Elevation and depression of the gun is controlled by a cross shaft and lever, convenient to the left hand of the driver and operated by the driver. A latch in the end of the lever permits the gun to be locked in any position of elevation or depression.

(2) In emergency, the gun may be manually fired by the bow gunner. Under all normal circumstances, however, the gun is electrically fired by the driver. Firing of the gun is accomplished by pressing buttons in the top of the Hycon controls, or by pulling back on the firing levers on the manual steering levers. In order to fire the gun, the main gun switch and gun safety switch on the instrument panel must be on (fig. 5) and the firing buttons must be operated simultaneously.

f. **Submachine Guns.** Two cal. .45 submachine guns are provided, one in the turret and one in the right-hand front sponson. They are usable through the turret and hull hatches, pistol ports, or may be used independently of the vehicle.

ARMAMENT

15. VISION DEVICES (figs. 1, 2 and 3).

a. Three periscopes, two mounted in the top of the turret and one in the turret hatch, provide indirect vision for personnel manning the turret. The 3-inch gunner's periscope is connected to the combination gun mount through a periscope parallel linkage. As the gunner turns the elevating handwheel, the periscope and guns are elevated or depressed at the same time and at the same angle. Thus, when the gunner adjusts the sight on the target, the guns are automatically aimed at the target. The telescopic sight is provided with elevation and deflection adjustments in order that the sight can be accurately synchronized with the 37-mm gun. This synchronization is accomplished by means of boresighting the gun and laying the telescopic sight on a common target. The two other periscopes in the turret are not linked to the gun mount, and both are rotated, raised and lowered by hand.

b. Two periscopes are provided in the bow of the vehicle, one for the driver and one for the bow gunner. The persicope used by the bow gunner is hooked by parallel linkage to the twin cal. .50 machine guns. As the gunner elevates or depresses the machine guns, the periscope is elevated or depressed simultaneously. Thus, when the gunner adjusts the sights on the target, the guns are automatically aimed at the target.

c. Heads of the periscopes are purposely made of a relatively fragile material. Thus, in case of a hit, they will shatter rather than become wedged into the mount, making removal and replacement possible without delay. To replace a shattered head, simply slide off the unserviceable head and slide a new head in its place.

d. To replace an unserviceable periscope, unlatch the safety lock, loosen the knurled nut and pull the periscope down by the handle. To install a serviceable unit, push it upward into the mount, tighten the knurled nut and secure it in place with the safety lock.

16. AMMUNITION STOWAGE.

a. At the time of preparation of this manual, the following stowage positions had been assigned for ammunition carried on the Heavy Tanks M6 and M6A1:

Ammunition	Stowage Position
Cal. .30, 5,500 rounds	4,000 in pocket in sponson in bow of vehicle. 1,500 in rack of turret.
Cal. .45, 1,200 rounds	In two boxes, one in pocket in sponson in bow of vehicle, and one in turret.

HEAVY TANKS M6 AND M6A1

Ammunition	Stowage Position
Cal. .50, 6,900 rounds	In rack in sponson at lower left rear corner of driving compartment. In rack in sponson at lower right center of driving compartment.
37-mm, 202 rounds	In rack in turret. In circular rack in turret.
3-in., 75 rounds	In rack in sponson at left and right center of driving compartment. In rack in turret.

b. Twenty-four hand grenades of various types are stowed in the driving compartment and in the turret.

Section IV

PREVENTIVE MAINTENANCE

	Paragraph
Purpose	17
Inspection at the halt	18
Inspection after operation	19
50-hour inspection	20
100-hour inspection	21

17. PURPOSE.

a. To insure mechanical efficiency, it is necessary that vehicles be systematically inspected at intervals in order that defects may be discovered and corrected before they result in serious damage.

b. Cracks that develop in castings or other metal parts may often be detected upon the completion of a run through the medium of dust and oil deposits.

c. Suggestions toward changes in design prompted by chronic failure or malfunction of a unit or group of units; pertinent changes in inspection or maintenance methods; and changes involving safety, efficiency, economy, and comfort should be forwarded to the office of the Chief of Ordnance, through technical channels, at the time they develop. Such action is encouraged in order that other organizations may profit thereby.

d. During operation, the driver should be alert to detect abnormal functioning of the engine. He should be trained to detect unusual engine sounds or noises. He should glance frequently at the instrument panel gages to see if the engine is functioning properly (fig. 7). An unsteady oil gage pointer indicates low oil pressure, if it occurs while engine speed is fairly constant. Unusually high engine speeds for given vehicle speeds, unusually high torque converter fluid temperatures or low fluid pressures, all indicate air in the converter system.

e. Only under exceptional circumstances should a vehicle be operated after indications of trouble have been observed. When in doubt, the engine should be stopped, and assistance obtained. Inspection during operation applies to the entire vehicle and should be emphasized throughout the driving instruction period.

18. INSPECTION AT THE HALT.

a. At each halt the operator should make a careful inspection of the vehicle to determine its general mechanical condition. Minor defects detected during the march, together with defects discovered at the halt, should be corrected before resuming the march. If the defects cannot be corrected during the halt, proper disposition of the vehicle should be made so that unnecessary delay may be avoided and major failure prevented.

b. A suitable general routine is as follows:

(1) Allow the engine to run a short time at idling speed (800 to 900 rpm). Listen for unusual noises. Stop the engine. Check converter pressure gage for immediate drop to zero.

(2) Walk around the vehicle, looking carefully for fuel or oil leaks.

(3) Examine tracks for adjustment and for worn, loose, broken, or missing parts.

(4) Inspect hull and fittings for missing, worn, or loose parts.

(5) Feel steering brake housings and gear case for evidence of overheating.

(6) Inspect the lights, if traveling at night with lights.

(7) Check the amount of fuel in the tank. Check fluid level in converter expansion tank.

(8) Wipe all windshields and vision devices. Do not use an oily or dirty rag.

19. INSPECTION AFTER OPERATION.

a. At end of day's operation, check the vehicle thoroughly to uncover damage, defects, or unsatisfactory conditions which may have developed during operation. Determine these at once, so that they can be corrected before the start of next operation. Cover all items noted in first echelon report except those relating to engine starting and performance. However, if any irregular or unsatisfactory performance of engine is observed during operation, make necessary checks and adjustments at this time, and report any work that will be required of company maintenance. Completeness of inspection at the end of operation is of vital importance in preparation of vehicle for the next operation. In addition, the more thoroughly the inspection is performed, the shorter will be the time required for prestarting inspection at start of next operation, and the more certain it will be that vehicle will go into operation in best possible combat condition.

PREVENTIVE MAINTENANCE   **TM 9-721**   **19**

b. A first echelon report on mechanical inspection will cover the following points:

(1) Engine oil level.
(2) Transmission oil level.
(3) Converter fluid level.
(4) Reduction gear housing oil level.
(5) Fuel strainer.
(6) Oil filters.
(7) Air cleaners.
(8) Fuel supply.
(9) Fire extinguishers.
(10) Voltmeter.
(11) Engine (starting).
(12) Starter.
(13) Primer.
(14) Engine oil pressure gage.
(15) Converter oil pressure gage.
(16) Final drive oil pressure gage.
(17) Transmission oil pressure gage.
(18) Engine (idling).
(19) Hand throttle.
(20) Tachometer.
(21) Engine (acceleration).
(22) Foot throttle.
(23) Ammeter.
(24) Cylinder temperature gage.
(25) Hycon pressure gage.
(26) Siren.
(27) Windshield wiper.
(28) Appearance.
(29) Steering.
(30) Lights: Dash, head, tail, stop.
(31) Leaks: Engine oil, transmission, differential, final drive, converter and Hycon system.
(32) Parts missing.
(33) Pioneer tools secure.
(34) Damage: Hull, fender.
(35) Tow cable.
(36) Tracks.
(37) Bogie wheels.
(38) Vertical links.
(39) Clevises.
(40) Armament.
(41) Manual steering levers.
(42) Speedometer.
(43) Odometer.
(44) Engine (cruising).
(45) Engine (speed).
(46) Engine (power).
(47) Remarks.

TM 9-721

HEAVY TANKS M6 AND M6A1

c. **Daily Report (Trip Ticket).**

MILEAGE TO DATE ....

U. S. A. No. .... DATE .... 194 ..

Organization ....

Dispatcher ....

TRIP NUMBER 1

Report to ....

Mileage in .... Hour of return ....

Mileage out .... Hour of departure ....

                                          Hours motor cut ....

Miles run .... Hours run ....

Nature of run ....

TRIP NUMBER 2

Report to ....

Mileage in .... Hour of return ....

Mileage out .... Hour of departure ....

                                            Hours motor cut ....

Miles run .... Hours run ....

Nature of run ....

TRIP NUMBER 3

Report to ....

Mileage in .... Hour of return ....

Mileage out .... Hour of departure ....

                                            Hours motor cut ....

Miles run .... Hours run ....

Nature of run ....

TOTAL MILES RUN .... TOTAL HOURS RUN ....

Accidents ....

....

FUELS AND LUBRICANTS ADDED: Gasoline .... Gal; Engine Oil .... Qt

Gear Oil .... Qt; Antifreeze .... Qt

Released .... (A. M.) (P. M.) : .... Signature

    NOTE: Fill in complete information at end of day's operation. Sign report and give it to the maintenance sergeant.

PREVENTIVE MAINTENANCE

TM 9-721
20

20. 50-HOUR INSPECTION.

a. General Instructions. At the end of every 50 hours of operation the maintenance personnel of the company will make a complete inspection of the vehicle. This inspection is intended to disclose all items which need repair or replacement. There may be a number of defects disclosed by this inspection which cannot be repaired or replaced by the company maintenance personnel. After required lubrication and cleaning, make all necessary repairs or replacements within the limits of tools and personnel training. It is the company's responsibility to inform higher maintenance echelons of repairs and replacements needed beyond its capacity.

b. Recommended Check List for Complete Inspection of Vehicle (50-hour Inspection).

ITEM TO BE INSPECTED	POSSIBLE DEFECT	OPERATION OR REMEDY
Inspector takes a position in front of vehicle		
(1) Towing shackle	Shackles or cotter pins missing	Replace
(2) Fenders	Torn or bent	Reweld or straighten
	Bolts loose or missing	Tighten or replace
(3) Siren cable	Damaged	Replace or repair
(4) Siren bracket	Broken or missing	Replace or repair
(5) Headlights	Burned out	Replace bulb
	Lens broken	Replace
	Cannot be removed	Repair catch
	Switch defective	Check connections, replace switch
(6) Headlight bracket	Broken or bent	Repair or straighten
Inspector moves to right side of vehicle		
(7) Sprocket	Mounting bolts loose or missing	Tighten or replace
	Cracked sprocket	Replace sprocket
(8) Connectors	Cracked, broken, or bent	Replace
	Worn	Replace
(9) Wedge nuts	Loose or damaged	Tighten all nuts or replace
(10) Track	Loose	Tighten
	Worn	Replace
	Dead block	Replace
(11) Bogie assemblies	Retaining screws loose or missing	Tighten or replace
(12) Volute spring	Broken or weak	Replace

TM 9-721
HEAVY TANKS M6 AND M6A1

ITEM TO BE INSPECTED	POSSIBLE DEFECT	OPERATION OR REMEDY
Inspector moves to right side of vehicle (cont.)		
(13) Support rollers	Grease leaks	Replace seal
	Cap screws, front and rear, loose, broken, or missing	Replace and lace with safety wire
	Grease fitting or relief valve damaged	Replace
(14) Bogie tires	Worn	Replace
	Grooved	Report
(15) Bogie wheels	Grease leaks	Replace seal, clean, loosen, or replace relief valve
(16) Track armor plate	Retaining screws loose or missing	Tighten or replace
(17) Hull rivets	Loose	Report
(18) Idler bracket rivets	Loose	Report
(19) Hubs, idler	Grease leaks	Replace seal
(20) Relief valves	Clogged with dirt	Clean, loosen, or replace
(21) Grease fittings	Clogged with dirt	Clean or replace
(22) Idler wheel	Damaged	Replace
(23) Idler adjustment	Damaged or loose	Replace or tighten
The above items are common to both sides of the vehicle		
Inspector moves to the rear of vehicle		
(24) Taillights	Wiring loose or defective	Repair
	Bulbs burned out	Replace
	Lens broken	Replace
	Switch defective	Check connections, replace switch
(25) Final drive units	Oil level low	Fill
	Cap screws loose or missing	Tighten or replace
	Drain plugs loose	Tighten
	Oil leaks	Replace gasket
Remove engine compartment top plate, and inspect engine, converter, transmission and final drive		
(26) Exhaust connections	Loose or missing	Tighten and replace
(27) Mufflers	Loose	Tighten brackets

PREVENTIVE MAINTENANCE

TM 9-721

Remove engine compartment top plate, and inspect engine, converter, transmission and final drive (cont.)

ITEM TO BE INSPECTED	POSSIBLE DEFECT	OPERATION OR REMEDY
(28) Priming lines	Leaks	Tighten or replace lines
	Broken lines	Replace lines
(29) Intake pipes	Loose. Possible breaks allowing dirty air to enter engine	Tighten or repair
(30) Ignition harness	Breaks in shielding	Solder
	Loose connections	Tighten
(31) Starter	Loose mounting bolts	Tighten
(32) Ground strap	Loose or broken	Tighten, repair, or replace
(33) Booster	Connections loose or damaged	Tighten or repair
	Leads damaged	Repair
	Poor spark	Replace
(34) Fire extinguisher horns	Clogged with dirt	Clean
	Loose connections	Tighten
(35) Rocker box covers	Oil leaks	Tighten nuts
(36) Junction boxes	Connections loose	Tighten
	Mountings loose	Tighten
(37) Fire extinguisher lines	Loose or damaged	Tighten or repair
(38) Oil cooler radiators	Dirty	Clean
(39) Fuel gage line	Leaks and loose	Repair and tighten
(40) Shroud bolts	Loose or missing	Tighten and replace
(41) Converter lines and fittings	Loose or damaged	Tighten or replace
(42) Converter fluid filter	Dirty or clogged	Clean, drain and flush
(43) Reduction gear case breather	Dirty or clogged	Clean, drain and flush
(44) Reduction gear oil filter	Dirty or clogged	Clean, drain and flush
(45) Gearshift lever rod connections	Loose, broken, or missing	Tighten or replace
(46) Converter retaining cap screws	Loose or missing	Tighten or replace

TM 9-721
HEAVY TANKS M6 AND M6A1

ITEM TO BE INSPECTED	POSSIBLE DEFECT	OPERATION OR REMEDY
Remove engine compartment top plate, and inspect engine, converter, transmission and final drive (cont.)		
(47) Transmission retaining cap screws	Loose or missing	Tighten or replace
(48) Final drive retaining cap screws	Loose or missing	Tighten or replace
Inspector inspects from top of vehicle		
(49) Gas tank filler cap covers	Covers missing	Replace
	Locking pins bent or otherwise defective	Repair
	Chain broken	Repair
(50) Engine compartment top plate and hatch covers	Bolts missing	Replace
	Hinges damaged	Repair
	Locking pins work hard	Repair
(51) Tow cable	Missing	Replace
Inspector removes engine compartment door and inspects engine		
(52) Engine oil filter	Clogged	Drain and flush
(53) Fuel strainer	Clogged	Drain and flush
(54) Connections to fuel pump	Loose or damaged	Tighten, repair, or replace
(55) Fuel pump mounting studs	Loose or damaged	Tighten, repair, or replace
(56) Connections to carburetor	Loose or damaged	Tighten, repair, or replace
(57) Connections to oil pump	Loose or damaged	Tighten, repair, or replace
(58) Connections to oil dilution	Loose or damaged	Tighten, repair, or replace
(59) Tachometer shaft	Loose or damaged	Tighten, repair, or replace
(60) Governor oil return line	Loose or damaged	Tighten, repair, or replace
(61) Oil pressure gage line	Loose or damaged	Tighten, repair, or replace
(62) Magneto breaker points	Burned	Replace if seriously burned
	Loose mounting	Tighten
	Dirty	Clean and oil
	Incorrect gap	Reset gap

PREVENTIVE MAINTENANCE

ITEM TO BE INSPECTED	POSSIBLE DEFECT	OPERATION OR REMEDY
Inspector removes engine compartment door and inspects engine (cont.)		
(63) Main oil screen	Dirty	Remove and clean
(64) Carburetor	Screen dirty	Remove and clean screen
	Improperly adjusted	Adjust
	Cracked	Replace
(65) Engine oil		Change while warm Prime system
(66) Engine accelerator	Engine spits or backfires	Adjust
(67) Priming lines	Loose or damaged	Tighten or replace
(68) Rocker box covers	Oil leaks	Tighten
(69) Accelerator linkage	Missing cotter pins	Replace
	Damaged rods	Replace
(70) Oil sump screen	Dirty	Remove and clean Clean sump
Inspector goes to driver's seat		
(71) Oil pressure (all gages)	Low or high	Stop engine Repair defect
(72) Voltmeter	Inoperative	Repair connections or replace
(73) Ammeter	Inoperative	Repair connections or replace
(74) Cylinder temperature gage	Inoperative	Repair connections or replace
(75) Hycon pressure gage	Inoperative	Repair connections or replace
(76) Fuel gage	Inoperative	Repair connections or replace
(77) Left magneto	Engine sputters or stops	Replace spark plugs Replace magneto
(78) Right magneto	Engine sputters or stops	Replace magneto Replace spark plugs
(79) Hycon controls	Loose or tight	Adjust
(80) Manual steering levers	Loose or tight	Adjust

HEAVY TANKS M6 AND M6A1

ITEM TO BE INSPECTED	POSSIBLE DEFECT	OPERATION OR REMEDY
Inspector goes to driver's seat (cont.)		
(81) Accelerator	No free play	Adjust
	Not free	Lubricate
(82) Hand throttle	Defective	Repair
(83) Transmission brake pedal	Not free	Adjust
(84) Gearshift lever	Inoperative	Repair
(85) Selector gearshift lever	Inoperative	Repair
(86) Lights	Inoperative	Replace bulbs
		Replace switches
		Replace wiring
(87) Fire detector light	Inoperative	Repair
(88) Siren	Inoperative	Repair or replace wiring
		Repair or replace switch
		Replace siren
(89) Oil temperature lines (all temperature gages)	Damaged or loose	Repair or tighten
(90) Oil pressure warning light	Inoperative	Repair
(91) Speedometer	Inoperative	Replace
(92) Speedometer cable	Loose or damaged	Tighten or repair
(93) Speedometer drive	Damaged grease fitting	Clean or replace
(94) Seats	Inoperative	Repair
		Lubricate
	Torn seats	Repair
Inspector removes battery box top plates		
(95) Batteries	Low water	Refill
	Lines corroded	Clean
	Terminal posts dirty or corroded	Clean
	Low specific gravity	Replace batteries

PREVENTIVE MAINTENANCE

TM 9-721
20-21

ITEM TO BE INSPECTED	POSSIBLE DEFECT	OPERATION
	Inspector inspects armament	
(96) Cal. .30 antiaircraft machine gun	Mount damaged	Repair or replace
(97) 3-inch gun and 37-mm gun	Cover missing	Replace
	Barrel damaged	Report
	Breech action poor	Repair
	Bore dirty	Clean
	Firing mechanism defective	Repair—clean gun
(98) Twin cal. .50 machine guns	Mount damaged	Repair or replace
(99) Bow cal. .30 machine gun	Mount damaged	Repair or replace

21. 100-HOUR INSPECTION.

a. A detailed inspection must be made at the end of each 100 hours of operation. Inspections should be made systematically, following a definite prearranged routine, to reduce time necessary to complete full vehicle inspection.

b. It is suggested a check sheet, based on the inspection operations contained in the following steps, be maintained. The crew chief will initial and sign the check sheet, signifying that inspections have been made and that repair operations, when necessary, have been satisfactorily performed.

c. Check sheet must then be posted to the service record of the vehicle involved and filed by vehicle and date separately from current records of the vehicle.

d. The following provides a list of inspections and corrective operations which must be performed at the 100-hour inspection:

(1) GENERAL. All inspections of hull, track suspension, and all other parts of the vehicle, excluding the engine, will be made by company maintenance. Any deficiencies which cannot be corrected will be listed.

(2) CLEANING. Vehicle will be cleaned inside and out by the company before delivering to unit maintenance shop. At least two members of the crew, one the driver, will assist maintenance mechanics.

(3) ENGINE OIL PRESSURE AND TEMPERATURE. Record following at 2,300 revolutions per minute and normal operating temperatures:

Oil pressure . . . . 65 to 75 lb
Oil temperature . . . . 160 F to 180 F

(4) CONVERTER OIL PRESSURE AND TEMPERATURE. Record following at 2,300 revolutions per minute and normal operating temperature:
Oil pressure .... 60 lb
Oil temperature .... 220 F to 260 F

(5) FINAL DRIVE OIL PRESSURE AND TEMPERATURE. Record following at 2,300 revolutions per minute and normal operating temperature:
Oil pressure .... 100 lb
Oil temperature .... 250 F
  Maximum .... 300 F

(6) CYLINDER TEMPERATURE. Record following at 2,300 revolutions per minute:
Cylinder temperature:
  Minimum .... 400 F
  Continuous operation .... 425 F
  Maximum .... 450 F

(7) HYCON PRESSURE. Record following before starting engine:
Hycon pressure tank pressure .... 1,500 lb

(8) FUEL AND OIL LEAKS. Remove engine compartment top guard and top plate (par. 48 b), and remove floor inspection plates and inspect all oil and fuel lines for leaks (with engine running and with engine stopped).

(9) ENGINE. Before working on engine be certain magnetos are grounded and battery switch is open.

(10) AIR CLEANERS. Inspect air cleaners. Have company clean if required.

(11) INSPECTION OF ENGINE.
(a) Engine Exterior. Clean the exterior of the engine thoroughly with SOLVENT, dry-cleaning, before removing any parts or covers, to prevent dirt from entering the engine.

(b) Fuel Leakage. Inspect the engine carefully for fuel leakage. The location of a leak may not always be where the fuel is found. Repair or replace any parts which are causing the fuel to leak.

(c) Fuel Connections. See that all fuel connections are tight. Replace any parts that cannot be tightened properly.

(d) Fuel System Strainer. Remove and clean the strainer.

(e) Carburetor Anchorage. See that the carburetor is securely fastened.

(f) Carburetor Controls. Check the carburetor controls for proper functioning, and lubricate all the joints and bearings.

(g) Accelerator. When the accelerator is advanced as far as it can go, no stress should be on the carburetor throttle stop.

PREVENTIVE MAINTENANCE

(h) Carburetor Fuel Strainer. Remove and clean the carburetor fuel strainer.

(i) Carburetor Air Screen. Remove and clean the carburetor air screen.

(j) Oil Leakage. Check for oil leakage. If any leakage is indicated, locate the leak and repair. Leakage oil may not always be at the point of origin. Possible locations are rocker box covers, push rod housing hoses, and oil connections.

(k) Oil Connections. See that oil connections are tight. Replace any part that cannot be tightened properly.

(l) Oil Sump Strainer. Wash the oil sump strainer.

(m) Magneto Lubricating Felt.

1. If the felt is soft and shows oil on the surface when squeezed between the fingers, no additional lubricant is needed. If this felt is dry, however, apply a small amount of oil to the portion of the felt attached to the cam follower main spring. Use just enough oil to make the felt soft so that oil can be brought to the surface by squeezing. Do not give it all it can hold. Lubricant of viscosity SAE 60 is suitable for average conditions. Whenever possible, choose a time for oiling when the engine and magneto are warm.

2. Never permit oil to reach the breaker contacts as it would cause pitting, rapid wear, and interference with operation. Keep the rest of the breaker mechanism clean and dry. Wipe the interior of the breaker housing. Check breaker assembly for pitting and burning at points. Replace if points are found to be pitted or burned. Wash clean before replacing the cover, but do not permit lint or other foreign matter to lodge on the contacts.

3. The ball bearings are packed in grease and need no additional lubricant between overhaul.

(n) Spark Plugs. Replace all spark plugs with new plugs or plugs reset with the proper gap.

(o) Ignition Harness. See that the ignition terminals are secure. The terminal nut should be snug. Care must be taken not to damage the nuts by overtightening. Check harness for chafing, oil leaks, and damaged shielding.

(p) Cylinder Fins. Inspect the fins of the cylinder which are accessible to make sure they are not plugged or coated with dirt. Fins should be kept clean so that they will radiate the heat in an efficient manner.

(q) Nuts and Cap Screws. Inspect all accessible nuts and cap screws to insure that they are tight and properly locked.

(r) Crankcase Breather Screen. Remove and clean the breather screen.

(s) Magneto Sump Plug. Inspect the magnetic sump plug for metal particles. Particles on the plug indicate possibilities of internal trouble, and should be reported to the ordnance maintenance officer.

(t) Compression. Check compression of each cylinder, removing the accessory-end spark plugs from all cylinders except the one being tested. If possible, use a pressure gage in place of one of the spark plugs in the cylinder being tested.

(u) Valve Clearances. Remove the rocker box covers and check the valve rocker clearances. Reset any clearances which are not within the specifications. The engine should be cold when checking or setting these clearances.

(v) Intake Pipes. Check the intake pipe packing nuts and cap screws. Do not tighten the intake pipe packing nuts at this inspection to remedy leaks, since such tightening may result in breaking the adhesive seal of the rubber packing. When the packing ring has once broken loose from the intake pipe or intake pipe boss, it will not adhere again. Tightening packing nuts at this inspection to remedy leaks may therefore result in increased leakage. If a leak is evident, the packing must be replaced. Do not operate an engine with leaking intake pipes. Tightening packing nuts after no more than 10 hours of operation on new rubber packing is permissible, because at this time the rubber packing is still soft and has not adhered to the nut. Leaking intake pipe packing is a fire hazard and a possible cause of improper mixture strength, and it is therefore recommended that the utmost caution be observed in following these recommendations.

(w) Exhaust System. Check the exhaust pipes, exhaust manifold and tail pipes for tightness and cracks. In order to reduce the possibility of difficulties arising from local overheating in the region of the exhaust port, care should be taken to tighten equally all exhaust flange stud attaching nuts. Exhaust leakage at this location caused by flange distortion or insecure fastening may result in burning of the exhaust port. CAUTION: Care should be exercised to avoid pulling the exhaust flange attaching nuts too tightly, and stripping the studs from the exhaust elbows.

(x) Push Rod Hoses. Check the push rod hoses and surrounding area for any evidences of oil leakage.

(y) Accessories. Check security of all accessories mounted on the engine accessory case, engine support beam, and brackets.

(12) OIL COOLER, ENGINE. Remove, drain, clean, and flush engine oil cooler. Allow to drain thoroughly before replacing. (Check for sticking bypass valve.)

(13) OIL COOLER, CONVERTER. Remove, drain, clean, and flush converter oil cooler. Allow to drain thoroughly before replacing.

PREVENTIVE MAINTENANCE

(14) OIL TANK. Drain and flush oil tank.

(15) INSPECT FUEL AND OIL LINES. Examine all oil and fuel line hose for worn or broken spots; flush oil lines, using low pressure air to blow through all lines to make sure they are not plugged.

(16) OIL FILTERS. Dismantle and clean all oil filters.

(17) FUEL FILTER. Disassemble and clean fuel filter.

(18) ENGINE COMPARTMENT.

(a) Check Following for Security:

1. Engine support bracket rivets.
2. Engine mounting bolts and brackets.
3. Engine shrouding in engine compartment.

(19) TORQUE CONVERTER. Drain and fill torque converter through filling and drain valve located above left engine compartment manhole in floor. Use hand pump when refilling.

(20) INSTALL ENGINE.

(a) Install engine (par. 49). Make sure that all connections are thoroughly tightened, and all conduits and lines are securely clamped in place to prevent chafing and kinking.

(b) Check exhaust pipe connections for security.

(c) Check all connections between air cleaner, air horn, and carburetor to see that they are dust tight.

(21) CONTROL LINKAGES. Check all linkages for free travel; clean, and oil. (Replace broken or missing cotter pins.)

(22) FILL OIL TANK. Fill oil tank.

(23) PRIME OIL PUMP. Prime engine oil pump by hand cranking while pouring oil into suction hose until one quart of oil is pulled into the engine.

(24) START ENGINE; ADJUST CARBURETOR.

(a) Open gas valves and start engine; if oil pressure does not show on gage in 10 seconds, shut down and reprime oil pump.

(b) After engine starts with proper oil pressure, warm for 10 minutes, observing all instruments and the engine for anything unusual.

(c) Adjust carburetor mixture control. Adjust idling speed for 400 revolutions per minute at carburetor. This does not infer that engine should be idled at this speed. Hand throttle will be set to idle engine at 800 revolutions per minute. This 400 revolutions per minute at carburetor allows easier gear shifting.

(25) TEST RUN VEHICLE, FINAL CHECKS.

(a) Take vehicle for test run; correct any deficiencies noted.

(b) Check engine compartment for leaks.

(c) Check engine oil level.

(d) Check converter oil level and oil pressure.

Section V
LUBRICATION

	Paragraph
Lubrication guide	22
Engine lubrication system	23
Torque converter lubrication system	24
Inspections	25
Trouble shooting	26
Reports and records	27

22. LUBRICATION GUIDE.

a. As a guide to regular and correct lubrication a guide is furnished with each vehicle. To assist in locating all lubrication fittings, they are painted red for easy identification.

23. ENGINE LUBRICATION SYSTEM.

a. **General** (fig. 8). In the engine lubrication system, the main oil supply is kept in a tank. Oil is drawn from the bottom of this tank by the engine oil pump, passed through a finger strainer and forced through the engine lubrication system. Oil returns to a sump which is emptied by a main and secondary scavenging line. Before returning to the engine oil tank, oil is forced through the automatically operated disk-type filter attached to the left side of the super-charger rear housing, and through the engine oil cooler. The amount of pressure built up in the system is determined by an oil pressure regulator valve located in the oil pump. The engine is vented by a crankcase breather located just back of the No. 1 cylinder. With this installation the oil tank is vented to the atmosphere.

b. **Oil Tank** (fig. 9). The oil tank is filled through a filler pipe on the top of the oil tank. The filler cover is equipped with a bayonet gage to indicate the amount of oil in the tank. A drain plug is located in the bottom of the oil tank.

c. **Oil Dilution Valve.** To assist in engine starting and warm-up in cold weather, an oil dilution valve permits engine oil to be thinned with gasoline. Oil is diluted before stopping engine, when low temperatures are anticipated. The oil dilution valve is solenoid operated, and is located on the right rear side of the engine beneath the right magneto (fig. 15). When open, the valve allows gasoline to flow through a line from the carburetor into the main oil inlet line, thus diluting the oil. The solenoid is operated by a toggle switch on the instrument panel (fig. 7). Since excessive oil dilution can cause a serious injury to the engine, the operating instructions on the instrument panel plate should be followed exactly. Check the oil dilution valve frequently to make sure the gasoline line is completely shut off when the switch is in the "OFF" position.

LUBRICATION

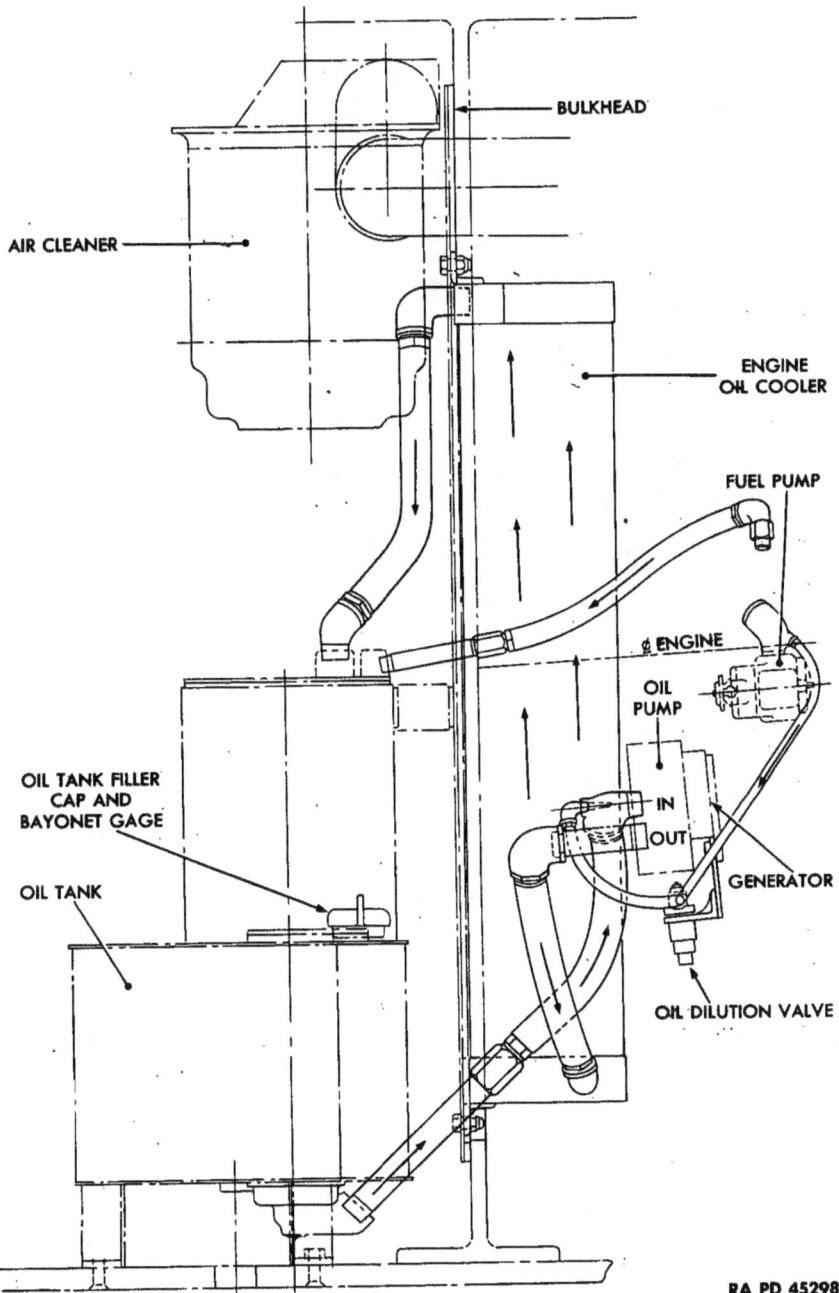

Figure 8 — Engine Oil Lines

TM 9-721
24 HEAVY TANKS M6 AND M6A1

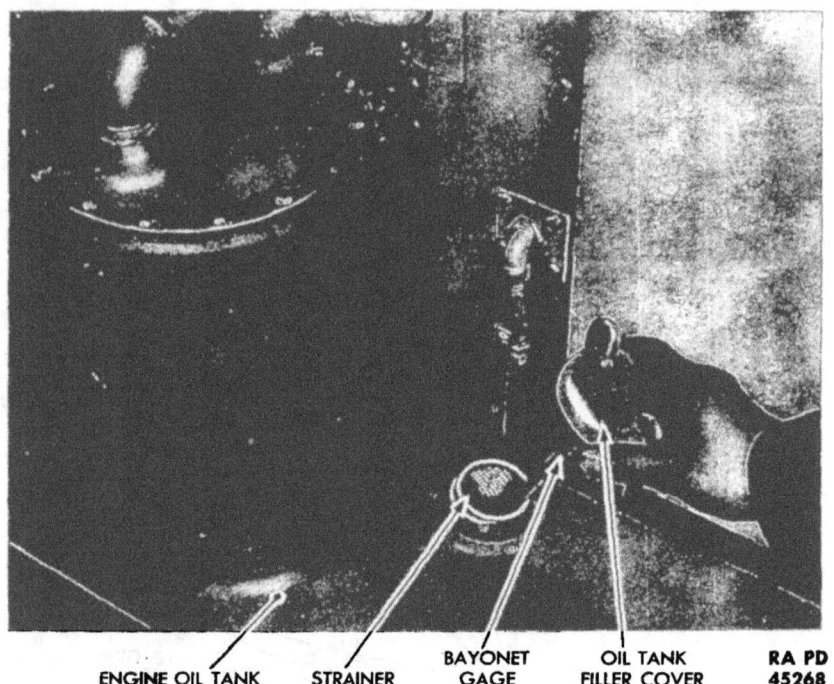

ENGINE OIL TANK — STRAINER — BAYONET GAGE — OIL TANK FILLER COVER — RA PD 45268

Figure 9 — Checking Engine Oil Supply with Bayonet Gage

24. TORQUE CONVERTER LUBRICATION SYSTEM (fig. 10).

a. Lubrication of the torque converter is provided from three separate sources. The pilot bearing located between the converter pump and turbine is lubricated by the operating fluid, and needs no attention. The duplex double row turbine bearing and the transmission input pinion roller bearing are lubricated by the transmission oil pump.

b. The oil supply for the torque converter reduction gear lubrication system is contained in a sump in the bottom of the reduction gear housing. Oil is drawn from the bottom of this sump by the reduction gear oil pump, and is forced through a filter and the reduction gearing. The oil returns to the sump as it is thrown off from the driving ring gear. A portion of the oil thrown from the driving ring gear reaches the auxiliary pump driving gear assembly, lubricating the gears and bearings there.

c. To relieve pressure from the reduction gear housing, a combination breather-filler cap oil level gage is mounted on the left side of the reduction gear housing.

d. The oil sump is filled through a filler pipe located on the left side of the reduction gear housing. A bayonet gage is mounted to the breather-

LUBRICATION

TM 9-721
24

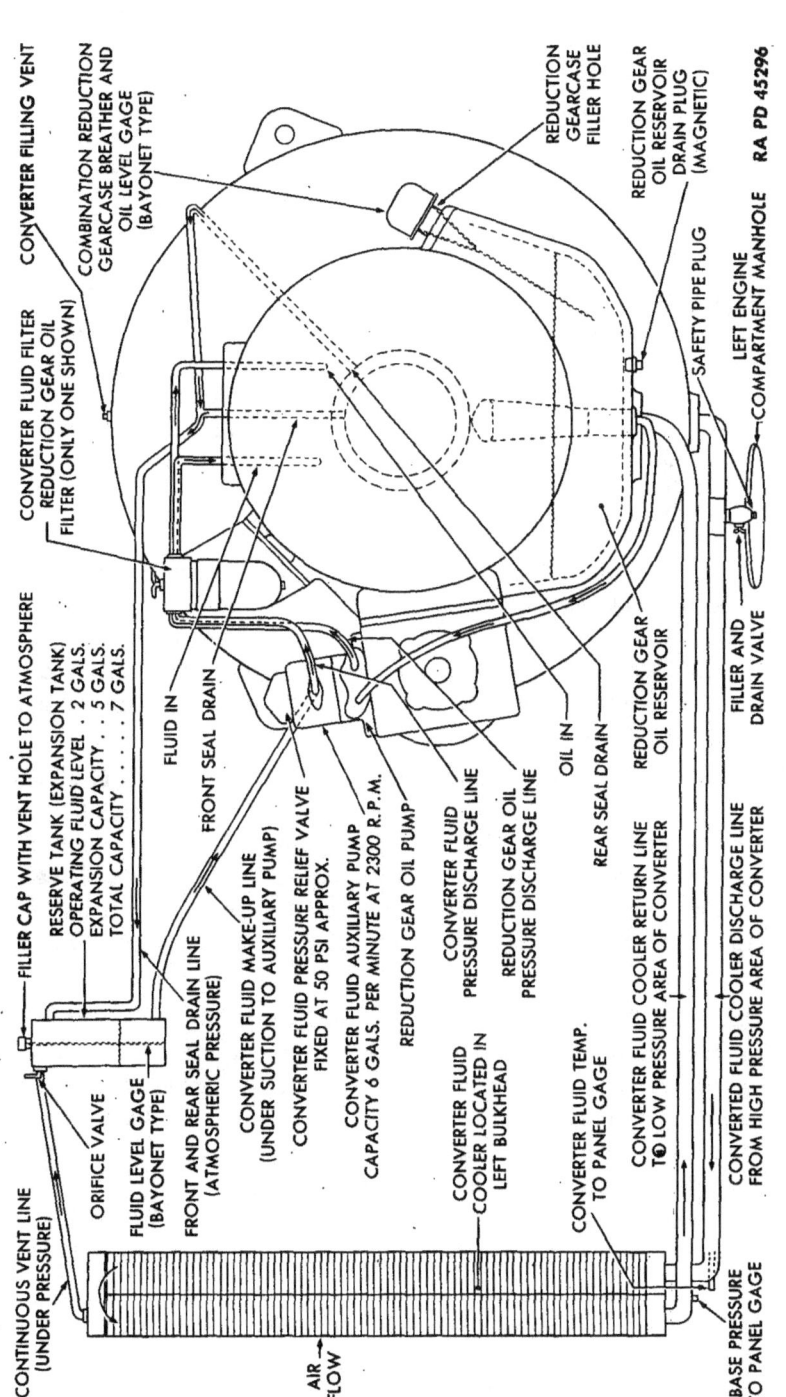

Figure 10—Torque Converter Fluid System

filler cap to indicate the amount of oil in the sump. Access to this gage is through the left rear engine compartment hatch cover. A magnetic drain plug is located in the bottom of the sump. To drain the sump it is necessary to remove the left engine compartment manhole in the floor.

e. The edge-type oil filter is self-cleaned by turning the handle on top of the cover one complete turn to the right. This must be done daily.

25. INSPECTIONS.

a. The entire lubrication system must be given regular periodic inspections to detect any leaks or damage to lines before it can cause loss of engine oil pressure. It is particularly important to check proper seating of the oil temperature gage bulb, since air leaks may develop at this point. Regular inspections of the lubrication system are included in the daily 50- and 100-hour periodic inspections (sec. IV).

26. TROUBLE SHOOTING.

a. **Testing Oil Pump Operation.** If no oil pressure is shown on the instrument panel gage, the action of the oil pump can be tested by disconnecting the oil inlet line at the oil filter. Prime the oil pump by pouring oil into the line. If the pump is operating properly, it will suck oil while the engine is being turned over with the starting motor. If no oil is drawn in, the pump must be replaced.

b. Check the oil pressure relief valve if the oil pump is in working order, and oil pressure is low; inspect the oil pressure relief valve. To inspect the valve, remove it from the oil pump body and look for dirt particles in the valve seat. This valve must be kept absolutely clean since even a minute dirt particle may hold the valve open, permitting oil from the supply line to be pumped back into the return line instead of into the engine.

c. **Special Precautions.** Too much emphasis cannot be placed upon the importance of tightening all oil line connections, and installing the oil temperature gage bulb securely so that any possible air leak into the lubrication system is eliminated. Extreme care should be taken to prevent dirt, sand, or other foreign material from entering the lubrication system, particularly when filling the oil supply tank. Watch the oil pressure gage on the instrument panel carefully at all times; if oil pressure is low at any time, stop the engine immediately and investigate the cause.

d. **Reference to Engine Trouble Shooting.** Because the lubrication system is so vital to engine operation, much of the trouble shooting procedure in the lubrication system has been included under engine trouble shooting (par. 47).

27. REPORTS AND RECORDS.

a. Reports. If lubrication instructions are closely followed, proper lubricants used, and satisfactory results are not obtained, a report must be made to the ordnance officer responsible for the maintenance of the materiel.

b. Records. A complete record of lubrication servicing will be kept for the materiel.

Section VI

CARE AND PRESERVATION

	Paragraph
Records	28
Cleaning	29

28. RECORDS.

a. Use. An accurate record must be kept of each motor vehicle issued by the Ordnance Department. For this purpose, the Motor Book for Ordnance Vehicles (O.O. Form 7255), generally called "Log Book," is issued with each vehicle and must accompany it at all times. This book furnishes a complete record of the vehicle from which valuable information concerning operation and maintenance costs, etc., is obtained, and organization commanders must insist that correct entries be made. Keep this book in a canvas cover to prevent its being damaged or soiled.

b. Assignment Record. Destroy the page bearing a record of assignment prior to entering the combat zone. Also delete all other references which may be posted regarding the identity of the organization.

29. CLEANING.

a. Grit, dirt, and mud are the sources of greatest wear to a vehicle. If deposits of dirt and grit are allowed to accumulate, particles will soon find their way into bearing surfaces, causing unnecessary wear, and, if the condition is not remedied, will soon cause serious difficulty. When removing engine parts or any other unit, in making repairs and replacements, or, if in the course of inspection, working joints or bearing surfaces are to be exposed, carefully remove all dirt and grit that might find its way to exposed surfaces. Keep tools clean, and always take care to eliminate the possibilities of brushing dirt or grit into the unit with sleeve or other part of the clothing. To cut oil-soaked dirt and grit, hardened grit, or road oil, use SOLVENT, dry-cleaning, applied with cloths (not waste) or a brush. Keep water away from the engine, as it might interfere with proper ignition and carburetion. Detailed information on cleaning is included in TM 9-850.

b. Open oilholes which have become clogged, using a piece of wire. Never use wood for this purpose, as splinters are likely to break off and permanently clog the passages. Particular care should be taken to clean and decontaminate vehicles that have been caught in a gas attack. See section IX for details of this operation.

Section VII

TOOLS AND EQUIPMENT

	Paragraph
Tools, accessories and equipment	30
Care of equipment	31

30. TOOLS, ACCESSORIES AND EQUIPMENT.

a. The following provides a complete list of tools, accessories and equipment carried on the Heavy Tanks M6 and M6A1.

(1) AMMUNITION AND ARMAMENT.

(a) Ammunition.

Cal. .30 .... 5,500 rounds
   80 percent A.P.
   20 percent tracer

Cal. .45 .... 1,200 rounds

Cal. .50 .... 6,900 rounds
   80 percent A.P.
   20 percent tracer

37-mm .... 202 rounds
   60 percent A.P. M51
   30 percent H.E. M74
   10 percent canister M2

3-inch .... 75 rounds
   80 percent A.P. M62
   20 percent H.E. M42

Grenades, hand 24
   Fragmentation M2 (8)
   Offensive M3 (w/fuse, detonation) (4)
   Smoke M8 (8)
   Thermite, incendiary (4)

(b) Armament.

GUN, machine, cal. .30, M1919A4 (flexible) 1
GUN, machine, cal. .30, M1919A4 1
GUN, machine, cal. .50, M2, HB (twin mount T-52) 2
GUN, 37-mm, M6 (T-49 combination mount) 1
GUN, 3-in., M7 (T-49 combination mount) 1
GUN, Thompson, submachine, cal. .45, M1928A1 2

(2) SIGHTING EQUIPMENT.
BINOCULAR, M3, complete, composed of:
   BINOCULAR, M3 (1)
   CASE, carrying (1)
   STRAP, neck (1)

HEADS, periscope, M8 and M6 12
PERISCOPE, M6 5
PERISCOPE, M6 (spare) 4
PERISCOPE, M8 (with telescope M15) 1
PERISCOPE, M8 (with telescope M15) (spare) 1
PRISMS, protectoscope 9

(3) ARMAMENT ACCESSORIES.
(a) Accessories, Cal. .30 Machine Gun.

BAG, empty cartridge, cal. .30 (A.A.) 1
BAG, empty cartridge, cal. .30 (flex. bow gun) 1
BELT, ammunition (250 rounds) 22
BOX, ammunition, cal. .30 (250 rounds) 16
BRUSH, chamber cleaning, M6 1
BRUSH, cleaning, cal. .30, M2 6
CAN, tubular, w/o contents 1
CASE, cleaning rod, M1 2
CASE, spare bolt, M2 (w/o contents) 4
CHEST, steel, M5 (w/o contents) 1
COVER, receiver, cal. .30 (A.A.) 1
COVER, receiver, cal. .30 (flex. bow gun) 1
COVER, spare barrel 2
COVER, tripod mount, M2 1
ENVELOPE, spare parts, M1 (w/o contents) 2
EXTRACTOR, ruptured cartridge, Mk. IV 2
MOUNT, tripod, machine gun, M2 1
MUZZLE, cover, cal. .30 (bow gun) 1
OILER, rectangular, 12-oz 1
REFLECTOR, barrel, cal. .30 1
ROD, cleaning, jointed, cal. .30, M1 2
ROLL, spare parts, M13 (w/o contents) 2
ROLL, tool, M12 (w/o contents) 2

(b) Accessories, Cal. .50 Machine Gun.

BAG, metallic belt link 1
BOX, ammunition, cal. .50, M2 66
BRUSH, cleaning, cal. .50, M4 8
CASE, cleaning rod, M15 2
CHUTE, metallic belt link 1
COVER, muzzle (twin cal. .50) 1
COVER, receiver (twin cal. .50) 1
COVER, spare barrel, M13, 45-in. 2
ENVELOPE, spare parts, M1 (w/o contents) 4
EXTRACTOR, ruptured cartridge 2

TOOLS AND EQUIPMENT

OILER, filling, oil buffer 1
ROD, jointed, cleaning, M7 2

(c) Accessories, Cal. .45 Submachine Gun.

BRUSH, chamber cleaning, M6 2
BRUSH, cleaning, cal. .45, M5 2
CASE, accessories and spare parts, M1918 (w/o contents) 1
COVER, Thompson submachine gun 2
ENVELOPE, fabric, one button, 3 x 3⅛ 1
MAGAZINE (30-round) (clip) 40
OILER, Thompson submachine gun 2
ROD, cleaning, cal. .45 2
SLING, gun, M1923 (Webbing) 2
THONG 2

(d) Accessories, 37-mm Gun.

BAG, empty cartridge (on T-49 mount) 1
BOOK, artillery gun, O.O. Form 5825 (blank) 1
BRUSH, bore, M8 1
CAN, ¼-gal 1
COVER, muzzle, 37-mm 1
COVER, breech 1
EXTENSION, oil gun 1
GUN, oil recoil 1
OIL, recoil, heavy, 1-qt 1
PIN, retaining 1
ROLL, spare parts, M13 1
SIGHT, bore 1
STAFF, cleaning, M5A1 1
TARGET, testing (set of 4) (not developed yet) 1

(e) Accessories, 3-inch Gun M7.

BOOK, artillery gun, O.O. Form 5825 (blank) 1
BRUSH, bore, M15, w/staff, consisting of:
  BRUSH, bore, M15 (1)
  STAFF, end (1)
  STAFF, middle (1)
CAN, ¼-gal 1
CASE, carrying, gunner quadrant M1 1
COVER, bore brush 1
COVER, breech 1
COVER, muzzle 1
EXTENSION, oil gun 1
GUN, oil, recoil 1
OIL, recoil, heavy, 1-qt 1

TM 9-721
30 HEAVY TANKS M6 AND M6A1

QUADRANT, gunner, M1 1
RAMMER, cleaning and unloading, M3 1
SETTER, fuse, M14 1
SIGHT, bore 1
TABLE, firing 1
TABLE, range and elevation 1
TARGET, testing (set of 4) (not developed yet) 1

(4) ARMAMENT SPARE PARTS.
(a) Spare Parts, Cal. .30 Machine Gun.
BAND, lock, front barrel bearing plug 1
BARREL 2
BOLT, group, consisting of: 2
  BOLT, assembly, B147299 (1)
  EXTRACTOR, assembly, C64135 (1)
  LEVER, cocking, D131317 (1)
  PIN, firing, assembly, C9186 (1)
  ROD, driving spring, assembly, B147222 (1)
  SEAR, C64137 (1)
  SPRING, driving, B212654 (1)
  SPRING, sear, assembly, A131265 (1)
COVER, assembly, group, consisting of: 1
  COVER, assembly, C9801 (1)
  LEVER, belt feed, B17503 (1)
  PAWL, feed belt, C8461 (1)
  PIN, belt feed pawl, assembly, B131255 (1)
  PIVOT, belt feed lever group, assembly, B110529 (1)
  SLIDE, belt feed, assembly, B131262 (1)
  SPRING, belt feed pawl, B147224 (1)
  SPRING, cover extractor, B17513 (1)
EXTENSION, barrel, assembly, group, consisting of: 1
  EXTENSION, barrel, assembly, C64139 (1)
  LOCK, breech, B147214 (1)
  PIN, breeck lock, assembly, B131253 (1)
  SPRING, locking barrel, B147230 (1)
FRAME, lock, assembly, group, consisting of: 1
  ACCELERATOR, C64142 (1)
  FRAME, lock, assembly, C9182 (1)
  PIN, accelerator, assembly, B131253 (1)
  PLUNGER, barrel, assembly, B131251 (1)
  PIN, trigger, A20503 (1)
  SPRING, barrel plunger, A135057 (1)
  SPRING, trigger pin, B147231 (1)
  TRIGGER, C8476 (1)

TOOLS AND EQUIPMENT

LEVER, cocking 1
LEVER, feed belt 1
PAWL, belt holding 1
PAWL, feed belt 1
PIN, accelerator, assembly 1
PIN, belt holding pawl split 1
PIN, cocking lever 1
PIN, firing, assembly 1
PIN, trigger 1
PLUG, front barrel bearing 1
SCREW, belt feed lever pivot 1
SPRING, barrel plunger 1
SPRING, belt feed pawl 1
SPRING, belt holding pawl 2
SPRING, cover extractor 1
SPRING, locking barrel 1
SPRING, sear, assembly 2
SPRING, trigger pin 1
TRIGGER 1
WASHER, lock, shakeproof 1

(b) Spare Parts, Cal. .45.

DISCONNECTOR 6D 1
EJECTOR, assembly (M1 only) 1
EJECTOR 4B (M1928A1 only) 1
EXTRACTOR 15A 1
PIN, firing, 14A 1
ROCKER 16D 1
SPRING, disconnector 9A 1
SPRING, firing pin 14C 1
SPRING, magazine catch 9D 1
SPRING, recoil 17C 1
SPRING, sear 9B 1

(c) Spare Parts, Cal. .50 Machine Gun.

BARREL, assembly 2
DISK, buffer 2
EXTENSION, firing pin 2
EXTRACTOR, assembly 2
LEVER, cocking 2
PIN, cotter, belt feed lever pivot stud 2
PIN, cotter, cover pin 2
PIN, cotter, switch pivot 3

PIN, firing 2
PLUNGER, belt feed lever 2
ROD, driving spring w/spring assembly 2
SLIDE, belt feed group, consisting of: 2
   ARM, belt feed pawl, B8914 (1)
   PAWL, feed belt, assembly, B8961 (1)
   PIN, belt feed pawl, assembly, B8962 (1)
   SLIDE, belt feed, assembly, B8965 (1)
   SPRING, belt feed pawl, A9351 (1)
SLIDE, sear 2
SPRING, belt feed lever plunger 2
SPRING, belt holding pawl 2
SPRING, cover extractor 2
SPRING, locking barrel 2
SPRING, sear 2
STUD, bolt 2

   (d) Spare Parts, 37-mm Gun M6.

EXTRACTOR, L.H. 1
EXTRACTOR, R.H. 1
GASKET, recoil cylinder filling plug 1
LEVER, firing pin cocking 1
LOCK, sear retaining 1
NUT, safety 1
PERCUSSION, mechanism, assembly, consisting of: 1
   GUIDE, firing pin, C77527 (1)
   PIN, firing, A25201 (1)
   PIN, straight, firing pin guide, BFDX1BG (1)
   SPRING, firing pin retracting, A25202 (1)
   STOP, firing spring, A196350 (1)
PIN, firing 1
PLUG, filling, recoil cylinder 1
PLUNGER, cocking lever 1
SPRING, cocking lever plunger 1
SPRING, firing 1
SPRING, firing pin retracting 1
SPRING, sear and trigger plunger 2
TRIGGER 1
TRIPPER, sear 1

   (e) Spare Parts, 3-inch Gun M7.

FORK, firing pin cocking 1
GASKET, recoil, cylinder filling plug 2

TOOLS AND EQUIPMENT   **TM 9-721**
                                                                30

PERCUSSION, assembly, consisting of: 1
   GUIDE, B163553 (1)
   PIN, A25829 (1)
   PIN, straight, BFDX1BK (1)
   SPRING, A25835 (1)
   STOP, A25634 (1)
PIN, cotter, 1/8 x 7/8 2
PIN, firing 1
PLUG, filling, recoil cylinder 2
PLUNGER, cocking fork 1
RETAINER, sear 1
SPRING, cocking fork plunger 1
SPRING, firing 1
SPRING, firing pin retracting 1
SPRING, sear 1

   (5) ARMAMENT TOOLS.
   (a) Tools, Cal. .30 Machine Gun.
SCREWDRIVER, common, 3-in. blade 1
WRENCH, combination, M6 1
WRENCH, socket, front barrel bearing plug 1
   (b) Tools, Cal. .50 Machine Gun.
WRENCH, combination, M2 1
   (c) Tools, 3-inch Gun M7.
EYEBOLT, breechblock removing 1
MALLET, rawhide, 23-oz 1
ROD, push 1
TOOL, breechblock, removing 1

   (6) ACCESSORIES AND EQUIPMENT, MISCELLANEOUS.
   (a) Equipment, Miscellaneous.
APPARATUS, decontaminating, 1½-qt 2
BAG, canvas field O.D., M1936 6
BAG, tool 1
BELT, safety 6
BOOK, O.O. Form 7255 1
BUCKET, canvas folding, w/spout, 8-qt 1
BULB, lamp inspection (24-30V) 1
CABLE, towing 1
CAN, ¼-gal (stencil "Oil Traverse and Stabilizer" in black letters
   ½ inch high on can) 1
CANTEEN, M1910, w/cup and cover, M1910 6
CHEK-CHART, lubrication 1
CONTAINER, water, 5-gal (Q.M.C. standard) 2

TM 9-721
30 HEAVY TANKS M6 AND M6A1

COVER, head lamp (removable)	2
CRANK, starting, w/extension and supports	1
EXTINGUISHER, fire, 4-lb, CO_2, portable	2
FLASHLIGHT (specification 17-197)	3
HELMET, tank (sizes in accordance with Q.M.C. head size chart)	6
INSTRUCTION (sheet for pioneer compass) (Mfgrs. Form 21-28)	1
KIT, first-aid (24 unit)	1
LAMP, inspection	1
MANUAL, field, cal. .30 M.G. M1919A4, FM 23-50	1
MANUAL, field, cal. .45 S.M.G. M1928A1, FM 23-40	1
MANUAL, field, cal. .50 M.G. M2, FM 23-65	1
MANUAL, field, for hand grenades, FM 23-30	1
MANUAL, instruction, for engine	1
MANUAL, spare parts, illustrated (for vehicle)	1
MANUAL, technical, for 37-mm Gun M6, TM 23-81	1
MANUAL, technical, for 3-in. Gun M7	1
MANUAL, technical, for stabilizer, TM 9-1798A	1
MANUAL, technical, for operator, TM 9-736A	1
MANUAL, technical, for power traverse	1
MAP, case board	
MITTENS, asbestos, pair	2
NET, camouflage, 45-ft x 45-ft	1
OIL, univis, No. 47	1
OILER (trigger-type, 1-pt)	1
PADLOCK, 1½-in., (2 keys)	1
ROLL, blanket	6
STOVE, cooking, M1941 (1 burner) consisting of:	1
(Coleman military burner No. 520, with accessory cups)	
TAPE, adhesive, 4-in. wide, 15-yd roll (blue)	1
TAPE, friction, ¾-in. wide, 30-ft roll	1
TAPE, rubber, ¾-in. wide, 30-ft roll	1
TARPAULIN, 12-ft x 12-ft	1
TUBE, flexible nozzle	2
WIPER, windshield	1

(b) Equipment, Signaling.

ANTENNA, complete w/cover (spare)	1
FLAG (set), M238, composed of:	1
CASE, CS90 (1)	
FLAG, MC-273 (red) (1)	
FLAG, MC-274 (orange) (1)	
FLAG, MC-275 (green) (1)	
STAFF, flag, MC-270 (3)	

TOOLS AND EQUIPMENT

FLARES 6
   WHITE, parachute, M17 (3)
   WHITE, cluster, M18 (3)
PANEL, signaling (12-ft x 2-ft 4-in.) (fluorescent neon red on one
   side, fluorescent white on the other) 1
PROJECTOR, ground signals, M4 1
RADIO (set), SCR-506 1
RADIO (set), either SCR-508 1
RATIONS
   Type "C" 2-day rations for 6 men .... 72 cans
   Type "D" 1-day rations for 6 men .... 2 cans

(c) Spare Parts, Vehicular.

BLOCK, track, with connectors 4
BULB, lamp, 3 CP 24-28V 4
PIN, cotter (for tow shackle pin) 2

(d) Tools, Pioneer.

AXE, (chopping, single bit, 5-lb) 1
CROWBAR, 5 ft long 1
HANDLE, mattock 1
MATTOCK, pick, M1 (without handle) 1
SHOVEL, short handle 1
SLEDGE, blacksmith, double face, 10-lb 1

(e) Tools, Vehicular.

ADAPTER, button head to bayonet-type 1
ADAPTER, button head to hydraulic-type 1
ADAPTER, ½ x 9/16 1
EXTENSION, handy grip, ½ sq drive, 5-in. 1
EXTENSION, ½ sq drive, 10-in. 1
CHISEL, cold 1
FILE, hand, smooth, 8-in. 1
FILE, 3 sq, smooth, 6-in. 1
FIXTURE, track connecting 2
GUN, grease hand, type 1 1
HAMMER, machinist, ball peen, 2-lb 1
HANDLE, combination tee, ½ sq drive, 11 in. long 1
HANDLE, combination tee, ¾ sq drive, 17 in. long 1
HANDLE, flexible, ½ sq drive, 12 in. long (w/cross bar) 1
HOSE, heavy-duty, button head-type, fitting 1
JACK (push and pull complete) 2
PLIERS, combination, slip joint, 8-in. 1
PLIERS, side cutting, 8-in. 1
RATCHET, reversible, ½ sq drive, 9-in. 1
SCREWDRIVER, machinist, 5-in. blade 1

SCREWDRIVER, special purpose, 1¾-in. blade	1
SCREWDRIVER, 1½-in. blade	1
SOCKET, head, ½ sq drive, ⅜-sq	1
SOCKET, head, ½ sq drive, 7/16 hex	1
SOCKET, head, ½ sq drive, ½ hex	1
SOCKET, head, ½ sq drive, 9/16 hex	1
SOCKET, head, ½ sq drive, ⅝ hex	1
SOCKET, head, ½ sq drive, ¾ hex	1
SOCKET, head, ½ sq drive, ⅞ hex	2
SOCKET, head, ½ sq drive, 15/16 hex	2
SOCKET, head, ½ sq drive, 1-in. hex	1
SOCKET, head, ½ sq drive, 1 1/16 hex	1
SOCKET, head, ½ sq drive, 1⅛ hex	1
SOCKET, head, ¾ sq drive, 1½ hex	1
SPEEDER, ½ sq drive, 17-in.	1
UNIVERSAL, joint, ½ sq drive	1
WRENCH, adjustable, single-end, 8-in.	1
WRENCH, adjustable, single-end, 12-in.	1
WRENCH, adjustable, single-end, 18-in.	1
WRENCH, engineer, double head, alloy steel, 5/16 x ⅜	1
WRENCH, engineer, double head, alloy steel, 7/16 x ½	1
WRENCH, engineer, double head, alloy steel, 9/16 x 11/16	1
WRENCH, engineer, double head, alloy steel, ⅝ x ¾	1
WRENCH, engineer, double head, alloy steel, 13/16 x ⅞	1
WRENCH, engineer, double head, alloy steel, 15/16 x 1	1
WRENCH, engineer, double head, alloy steel, 1 1/16 x 1¼	1
WRENCH, engineer, double head, alloy steel, 1⅛ x 1⅜	1
WRENCH, safety screw, 3/32 hex	1
WRENCH, safety screw, ⅛ hex	1
WRENCH, safety screw, 3/16 hex	1
WRENCH, safety screw, ¼ hex	1
WRENCH, safety screw, 5/16 hex	1
WRENCH, safety screw, ⅜ hex	1
WRENCH, safety screw, 9/16 hex	1
WRENCH, safety screw, ⅝ hex	1

31. CARE OF EQUIPMENT.

a. An accurate record of all tools, accessories, and equipment should be kept in order that their location and condition may be known at all times. Items becoming lost or unserviceable should be replaced immediately. All tools and equipment should be cleaned and in proper condition for further use, before being returned to their location. Care must be used in fastening the tools carried on the outside of the vehicle, and frequent inspections and oiling are necessary to prevent corrosion.

Section VIII

OPERATION UNDER UNUSUAL CONDITIONS

	Paragraph
Cold weather operation	32
Cold weather accessories	33
Operation at high temperature	34
Desert operation	35

32. COLD WEATHER OPERATION.

a. General. The operation and maintenance at low temperatures involve factors which do not exist at normal temperatures, and operators and maintenance personnel must spend more time in protective maintenance. Failure to give this extra service will result in actual damage, unnecessary and unwarranted expense, and failure to start.

b. Temperature Ranges. Low temperatures have been divided into two ranges, minus 10 F to minus 30 F, and below minus 30 F. Engines and lubricants undergo changes in their physical properties below minus 30 F. In many cases, accessory equipment for supplying heat to engine, fuel, oil, and intake air is required. Engine and vehicular lubrication at temperatures above minus 10 F is covered in the lubrication section of this manual (sec. V) and in the lubrication guide furnished with the vehicle. The instructions in the following subparagraphs are intended to supplement this information, and apply only to instances where the temperature falls below minus 10 F for extended periods.

c. Protective Maintenance.

(1) The greatest dangers in cold weather engine starting and operation arise from lubrication failures due to thickened oil, slow or blocked circulation of oil, and improper or too frequent use of oil dilution valve.

(2) Whenever possible, keep the vehicle in a heated enclosure when it is not being operated. Always use the protection of a shed or other enclosed space if available. During a halt, or overnight stop, if enclosed space is not available, close the engine compartment as tightly as possible, and cover the rear of the vehicle with tarpaulin.

(3) In extremely cold weather, remove oil from the vehicle during overnight stops and keep oil in a warm place until vehicle is to be operated again. If warm storage is not available, heat the oil before installing in the vehicle. (Avoid overheating the oil; heat only to the point where the bare hand can be inserted without burning.) *Tag the vehicle in a conspicuous place in the driving compartment to warn personnel that crankcase is empty.*

(4) If the vehicle is to be kept outdoors, and if the oil cannot be drained, cover the engine with a tarpaulin. About 3 hours before the engine

is to be started, place fire pots under the tarpaulin. *Use only accepted, flame-covered preheating units.* It is also important to assist the warming of the engine compartment by means of the auxiliary generating unit and heater.

(5) Be careful in operating oil dilution valve. Make sure that it is functioning properly and follow the directions given on the instruction plate located on the instrument panel.

d. Engine Starting.

(1) Prior to attempting to start, see that everything is in readiness so that the engine will start on the first trial. Try to avoid letting the engine fire a few times, and then stop. Water is one of the products of combustion. In a cold engine, this water may form a frost and make it impossible to start without heating the engine to above 32 F. Prolonged efforts to start will wear down the batteries.

(2) When attempting to start, turn the engine over as rapidly as possible. Every engine has a critical cranking speed, that is, the engine must be turned over at a certain rate of speed before any start at all is possible. Below this speed, the fuel pump will not deliver fuel fast enough to keep th engine running.

(3) After the engine has started, follow the warm-up instructions given in section II, paragraphs 9 and 10.

33. COLD WEATHER ACCESSORIES.

a. A number of the most common accessories used in starting engines in cold weather are listed below. The use of the accessories is not mandatory. They are given only as suggestions and are to be employed at the discretion of the officer in charge of the materiel.

(1) Tarpaulins, tents, or collapsible sheds are useful for covering vehicles, particularly the engines.

(2) Accepted preheating units will aid materially in heating the engine.

(3) Extra batteries and facilities for changing batteries quickly are aids in starting.

(4) Steel drums and suitable metal stands are useful for heating oil.

(5) Insulation of the fuel lines will prevent ice formation inside the lines.

(6) It is often necessary to cut the center out of the track shoes for operation in snow. Snow and ice have a tendency to become packed between sprocket and track. This will cause the track to be thrown unless the snow and ice can be pushed out through holes cut in the shoe.

OPERATION UNDER UNUSUAL CONDITIONS

34. OPERATION AT HIGH TEMPERATURE.

a. Due to the fact the engines used in the Heavy Tanks M6 and M6A1 are air-cooled, the high temperature of the vicinity in which the vehicles are operating will necessarily reflect an increase in all engine and vehicular temperatures. Watch engine, converter, and final drive temperature gages carefully.

(1) The following lists the maximum temperatures of engine and vehicular components beyond which trouble may be expected:

Oil inlet temperature	200 F
Cylinder temperature (normal rated power to 90 percent rated power, one-hour operation)	450 F
Converter oil temperature	300 F
Final drive oil temperature	300 F

35. DESERT OPERATION.

a. Desert operation and operation under other extremely sandy road conditions may necessitate cleaning the air cleaners as often as every 4 hours.

Section IX

MATERIEL AFFECTED BY CHEMICALS

	Paragraph
General	36
Protective measures	37
Decontamination	38
Special precautions for automotive materiel	39

36. GENERAL.

a. Gas clouds, chemical shell, and chemical spray are the major chemical warfare methods for destroying or damaging materiel. Removing or destroying the dangerous liquid or solid chemical agents spread by these methods, or changing these chemical agents to harmless substances is called decontamination.

37. PROTECTIVE MEASURES.

a. When materiel (except ammunition) is in constant danger of attack with chemicals, apply a light coat of engine oil to unpainted metal parts. Take care that the oil does not touch the optical parts of instruments, or leather or canvas fittings. Protect materiel not in use with covers as far as possible. Keep ammunition in sealed containers.

b. Ordinary fabrics offer practically no protection against mustard gas or lewisite. Rubber and oilcloth, for example, will be penetrated within a short time. The longer the period of exposure, the greater the danger, when apparel made of either of these materials is worn. Rubber boots contaminated with mustard gas may offer a grave danger to men who wear them several days after the attack. Impermeable clothing, designed to prevent penetration of chemicals, will resist penetration almost indefinitely, but the maximum time such clothing can be worn is from 5 to 10 minutes in summer and about 30 minutes in winter.

38. DECONTAMINATION.

a. For the removal of liquid vesicants (mustard, lewisite, etc.) from materiel, the following steps should be taken:

b. **Protection of Personnel.**

(1) For all of these operations a service gas mask and a complete suit of protective clothing, either permeable or impermeable, depending upon the type of contamination, must be worn. Immediately after removing the suit, a thorough bath with soap and water (preferably hot) must be taken. If any skin areas have come in contact with liquid or vapor mustard gas, or if the vapor of mustard has been inhaled, it is imperative that complete first-aid measures be given within 5 minutes to be effective as a

preventive. First aid must be prompt for little can be done later than 20 to 30 minutes after exposure.

(2) Casualties caused by vesicants (mustard, lewisite, etc.) or by lung irritants (phosgene, all vesicants, etc.) should be immediately removed from the contaminated area.

(a) Vesicant Casualties. Remove the contaminated clothing. If the face has been exposed, wash the eyes and rinse the nose and throat with a saturated boric acid, weak sodium bicarbonate, or common salt solution. Mustard burns or skin areas wet with liquid mustard should be immediately and repeatedly swabbed with a solvent, such as kerosene, any oil, alcohol, or with **CARBON TETRACHLORIDE**. Then wash thoroughly with soap and water.

(b) Lung Irritant Casualties. To reduce his oxygen requirements, make the casualty lie down. Keep him warm and give him nonalcoholic stimulants such as hot coffee or tea. He should be evacuated as soon as possible as an absolute litter case.

(c) Complete first-aid instructions to supplement the above general instructions are contained in **FM 21-40**.

(3) Decontaminate garments exposed to vesicants. If impermeable clothing has been exposed to vapor only, it may be decontaminated by hanging in the open air, preferably in sunlight, for several days. It may also be cleaned by steaming for 2 hours. If impermeable clothing has been contaminated with liquid vesicant gases, steam it for 6 to 8 hours. Various kinds of steaming devices can be improvised from equipment available in the field.

c. Procedure.

(1) Commence by freeing materiel of dirt through the use of sticks, rags, etc. Sticks, rags, and other cleaning items used in decontamination must be burned or buried immediately after their use.

(2) If the surface of the materiel is coated with grease or heavy oil, remove it before decontamination is begun. For this cleaning use **SOLVENT**, dry-cleaning, or other available solvents for oil, applied on rags attached to the ends of sticks.

(3) Decontaminate the painted surfaces of the materiel with bleaching mixture made by mixing equal parts by weight of **AGENT**, decontaminating (chloride of lime), and water. So large a proportion of bleaching powder is added to the water that only a small part is dissolved; therefore a suspension, or "slurry" is formed. This slurry should be swabbed over all surfaces. Wash off thoroughly with water, then dry and oil all surfaces.

(4) All unpainted metal parts of materiel that have been exposed to any gas except mustard and lewisite must be cleaned as soon as

possible with SOLVENT, dry-cleaning, or ALCOHOL, denatured, and wiped dry. All parts should then be coated with oil.

(5) All unpainted metal parts and instruments exposed to mustard or lewisite must be decontaminated with AGENT, decontaminating, noncorrosive, mixed 1 part solid to 15 parts solvent (ACETYLENE TETRACHLORIDE) by weight. If this is not available, use warm water and soap. Bleaching slurry must not be used because of its corrosive action on unpainted metal parts. After decontamination, wipe all metal surfaces dry and coat them lightly with engine oil, except the surfaces of small arms, which must be coated with OIL, lubricating, preservative, light. Instrument lenses may be cleaned only with PAPER, lens, tissue, using a small amount of ALCOHOL, ethyl.

(6) If AGENT, decontaminating (chloride of lime), is not available, materiel may be temporarily cleaned with large volumes of hot water. However, mustard gas lying in joints or in leather or canvas webbing is not removed by this procedure and will remain a constant source of danger until the materiel can be properly decontaminated. Because all mustard gas washed from materiel lies unchanged on the ground, the area should be plainly marked with warning signs before abandonment.

(7) Leather or canvas webbing that has been contaminated should be scrubbed thoroughly with bleaching slurry. If this treatment is believed insufficient, it may be necessary to burn or bury such materiel.

(8) Ammunition which has been exposed to vesicant gas must be thoroughly cleaned before firing. To clean ammunition use AGENT, decontaminating, noncorrosive; or if this is not available, strong soap and warm water. After cleaning, wipe all ammunition dry with clean rags. *Do not use dry powdered AGENT, decontaminating (chloride of lime) (used for decontaminating certain types of materiel on or near ammunition supplies)*, as flaming occurs when it touches liquid mustard.

(9) Detailed information on decontamination is contained in FM 21-40 and TM 3-220.

39. SPECIAL PRECAUTIONS FOR AUTOMOTIVE MATERIEL.

a. When a vehicle has been subjected to gas attack with the engine running, service the air cleaner by removing the oil, flushing with SOLVENT, dry-cleaning, and refilling with the proper grade of oil.

b. Instrument panels should be cleaned in the same manner as instruments.

c. Discard contaminated seat cushions.

d. Washing the compartments thoroughly with bleaching slurry is the most that can be done in the field. In warm weather, operators should constantly be on the alert for slow vaporization of the mustard or lewisite.

e. Decontaminate the exterior surfaces of the vehicle with bleaching slurry. Repainting may be necessary after this operation.

PART TWO — Organization Instructions

Section X

GENERAL INFORMATION ON MAINTENANCE

	Paragraph
Organization maintenance	40

40. ORGANIZATION MAINTENANCE.

a. Scope. The scope of maintenance and repair by the crew and other units of the using arms is determined by the availability of suitable tools, availability of necessary parts, capabilities of the mechanics, time available, and the tactical situation. All of these are variable and no exact system of procedure can be prescribed.

b. Allocation of Maintenance. Indicated below are the maintenance duties for which tools and parts have been provided for the using arm personnel. Other replacements and repairs are the responsibility of ordnance maintenance personnel but may be performed by using arm personnel when circumstances permit, within the discretion of the commander concerned. Echelons and words as used in this list of maintenance allocations are defined as follows:

SECOND ECHELON: Line organization regiments, battalions, companies, detachments, and separate companies.

THIRD ECHELON: Ordnance light maintenance companies, ordnance medium maintenance companies, ordnance divisional maintenance battalions, and post ordnance shops.

FOURTH ECHELON: Ordnance heavy maintenance companies, and service command shops.

FIFTH ECHELON: Ordnance base regiments, ordnance bases, arsenals, and and manufacturers' plants.

SERVICE (Including preventive maintenance): Refer to AR 850-15, paragraph 23 a (1) and (2). Consists of servicing, cleaning, lubricating, tightening bolts and nuts, and making external adjustments of subassemblies or assemblies and controls.

REPLACE: Refer to AR 850-15, paragraph 23 a (4). Consists of removing the part, subassembly or assembly from the vehicles and replacing it with a new or reconditioned or rebuilt part, subassembly or assembly, whichever the case may be.

TM 9-721
40   **HEAVY TANKS M6 AND M6A1**

REPAIR: Refer to AR 850-15, paragraph 23 a (3) and (5), in part. — Consists of making repairs to, or replacement of the part, subassembly or assembly, that can be accomplished without completely disassembling the subassembly or assemblies, and does not require heavy welding, or riveting, machining, fitting and/or alining or balancing.

REBUILD: Refer to AR 850-15, paragraph 23 a (5), in part, and (6). — Consists of completely reconditioning and replacing in serviceable condition any unserviceable part, subassembly or assembly of the vehicle, including welding, riveting, machining, fitting, alining, balancing, assembling and testing.

NOTE: Operations allocated to the echelons as indicated by "E" may be accomplished by the respective echelons in emergencies only.

BOXES, RACKS, AMMUNITION
Boxes, ammunition .... Replace
Racks, ammunition .... Replace

CONTROLS, BRACKETS AND LEVERS
Bearings, clutch release .... Replace
Brackets and levers .... Replace
Controls and linkage .... Replace

ELECTRICAL SYSTEM
Battery .... Replace, recharge
Box, apparatus (generator control) .... Replace
Box, terminal .... Replace
Box terminal breaker .... Replace
Box, turret, collector ring .... Replace
Brackets, mounting and support .... Replace
Cables, battery .... Replace
Conduit .... Replace
Filters, generator .... Replace
Generator, auxiliary, assembly .... Replace
Lamps (all) .... Replace, service
Mechanism, traversing, turret .... Replace
Siren .... Replace
Solenoids .... Replace
Switches .... Replace
Wires (all) .... Replace

ENGINE, RADIAL—WRIGHT G-200
Baffles and cowling .... Replace
Carburetor assembly .... Replace
*Engine assembly .... Replace (*)
Flywheel and fan assembly .... Replace (E)
Generator assembly .... Replace

---
* The second echelon is authorized to remove and install engine and transmission assemblies, transfer unit controlled differential assembly and other items marked by asterisk (*). However, when it is necessary to replace an item marked by an asterisk with a new or rebuilt part, subassembly or unit assembly, the assembly marked by asterisk will not be removed from the vehicle by the second echelon until authorization is received from a higher echelon.

GENERAL INFORMATION ON MAINTENANCE

Harness, ignition .... Replace
Magneto assembly .... Replace, repair (E)
Manifold, exhaust .... Replace
Pipe, intake .... Replace
Plugs, spark .... Replace
Plugs, spark (2-piece) .... Repair (E)
Pump assembly, fuel .... Replace
Pump assembly, oil .... Replace
Rocker assembly, valves .... Replace (E), repair (E)
Rods, valve push .... Replace
Solenoid, carburetor shut-off .... Replace
Starter assembly .... Service, replace
Strainer, oil .... Service, replace

EXTINGUISHING SYSTEM, FIRE
Controls, remote .... Replace
Cylinders .... Replace
Lines and nozzles .... Replace

FUEL SYSTEM
Filters .... Replace
Lines, valves, fittings .... Replace
Lines, valves, fittings .... Repair (E)
Tank, fuel .... Replace (E)

HULL ASSEMBLY
Cleaners, air .... Replace
Detectors, flame .... Replace
Doors and enclosure plates .... Replace
Door, escape .... Replace
Guards, mud .... Replace
Insulation and padding .... Replace
Mounting, periscope .... Replace
Muffler and bracket assembly .... Replace
Periscope .... Replace
Seats .... Replace

INSTRUMENTS AND PANELS
Instruments .... Replace
Panels and connections .... Replace

LINES, OIL
Engine .... Replace

LUBRICATION SYSTEM
Filter, engine .... Replace
Filter, torque converter .... Replace
Filter, torque converter reduction .... Replace
Filter, transmission .... Replace
Tank, oil reserve .... Replace

HEAVY TANKS M6 AND M6A1

MECHANISM, AUXILIARY, STEERING
Cylinder, booster, steering brake .... Replace
Lines and connections .... Replace
Pedestal, cylinder, return .... Replace
Spring assembly .... Replace

SUSPENSION ASSEMBLY, TRACK
Bearings and seals, bogie and idler wheels .... Replace
Bogie components .... Replace
Bracket, idler .... Replace (E)
Roller and bracket assembly, track supporting .... Replace
Track assembly .... Replace, repair
Wheels, bogie .... Replace
Wheels, idler .... Replace

TORQUE CONVERTER, TRANSMISSION, AND FINAL DRIVE UNITS
Brake, steering .... Replace
Control, components (external) .... Replace
*Converter, torque and transmission assembly .. Replace(*), repair(*)
Drive assembly, final .... Replace
Hub or sprockets .... Replace

TURRET ASSEMBLY
Mechanism, traversing, manual .... Replace
Seats .... Replace

VEHICLE ASSEMBLY
Tank assembly .... Service, preventive maintenance

---

* The second echelon is authorized to remove and install engine and transmission assemblies, transfer unit controlled differential assembly and other items marked by asterisk (*). However, when it is necessary to replace an item marked by an asterisk with a new or rebuilt part, subassembly or unit assembly, the assembly marked by asterisk will not be removed from the vehicle by the second echelon until authorization is received from a higher echelon.

Section XI

TOOLS AND EQUIPMENT

	Paragraph
Organization tools	41
Fire extinguishing system	42

41. ORGANIZATION TOOLS.

a. **Crew Tools and Equipment.** The tools and equipment ordinarily required for operations performed by the using arms (first echelon) are included as regular equipment with each vehicle, and are listed in section VII.

b. **Company Tools and Equipment.** The tools and equipment ordinarily required for vehicle inspection and maintenance in the field include many items not used by the crew and are not provided with each vehicle. They are a regular part of company equipment and material to be used on all vehicles in the company.

c. **Regimental Tools and Equipment.** A still more extensive group of regular and special tools and special equipment is provided for use of the regimental maintenance unit. They cover all the requirements of first and second echelon maintenance.

d. **Care of Tools and Equipment.** An accurate record of all tools and equipment should be kept in order that their location and condition may be known at all times. Items becoming lost or unserviceable should be immediately replaced. All tools and equipment should be cleaned and in proper condition for further use before being returned to their location. Care must be used in fastening the tools carried on the outside of the vehicle, and frequent inspection and oiling are necessary to prevent corrosion.

42. FIRE EXTINGUISHING SYSTEM.

a. **Description.**

(1) The fire extinguishing system consists of a supply of carbon dioxide gas stored in 6 cylinders, each having a capacity of 10 pounds of carbon dioxide; manual release control for operation of the cylinders; and tubing to convey the gas to the engine compartment. The tubing is terminated in shielded discharge nozzles which effectively distribute the gas. The cylinders are mounted in the right sponson, midway between the front and rear of the vehicle (fig. 12). Access to the cylinders for maintenance operations is provided by a compartment plate in the right track armor plate (fig. 11).

(2) The cylinders are connected to the supply tubing by means of a double check tee, which tee prevents the loss of gas into engine compartment should three of the cylinders be operated while the other cylinders are removed for weighing or recharging.

(3) In addition to the built-in or fixed system for the engine com-

TM 9-721
42 HEAVY TANKS M6 AND M6A1

FIXED FIRE EXTINGUISHER COMPARTMENT PLATE — ARMOR PLATE (RIGHT SIDE OF VEHICLE) — RETAINING SCREWS — RA PD 45300

Figure 11—Fixed Fire Extinguisher Compartment Plate

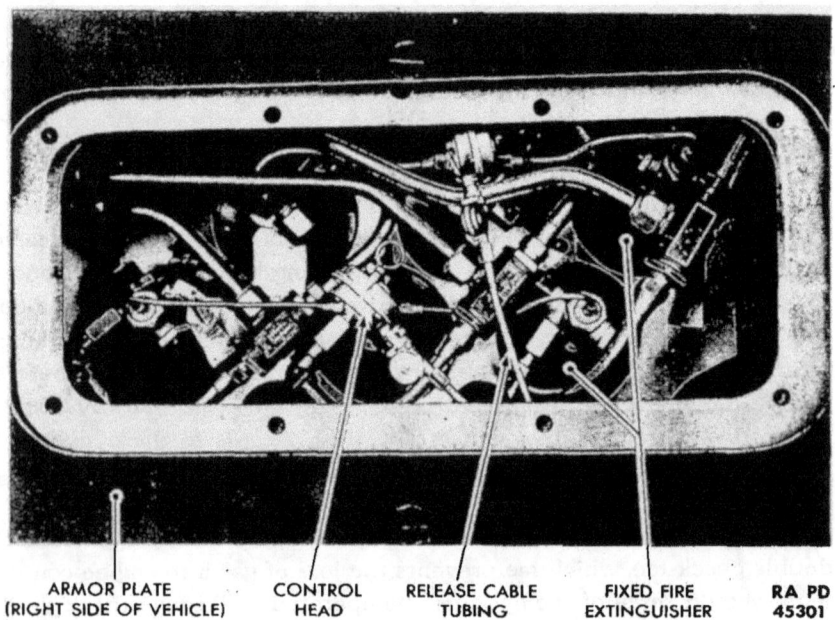

ARMOR PLATE (RIGHT SIDE OF VEHICLE) — CONTROL HEAD — RELEASE CABLE TUBING — FIXED FIRE EXTINGUISHER — RA PD 45301

Figure 12—Installation of Fixed Fire Extinguishers

TOOLS AND EQUIPMENT

TM 9-721
42

Figure 13 — Right Front Corner of Driving Compartment

partment, two 4-pound portable extinguishers are provided for small fires in or about the vehicle. One is located in the turret, and the other in the driving compartment. Full operating instructions are found on the extinguisher name plate.

b. Operation.

(1) The fire extinguishing system is entirely manual in operation. It is imperative, therefore, that there be as little delay as possible in discharging the gas, as its effectiveness is greatly increased by catching the fire in the beginning.

(2) The system may be put into operation from the outside of the vehicle, or from within the driving compartment. Two fire extinguisher release handles are mounted inside the driving compartment on the right side of the hull directly behind the mount for the bow cal. .30 machine gun (fig. 13). The two fire extinguisher release handles are mounted outside the vehicle on the right side of the hull (fig. 14). To operate the system, merely pull out on the release handles. The further the handle is pulled out (within limits) the faster the gas will be released. Each handle operates to discharge 3 cylinders. Do not open second 3 cylinders except in emergency, and then only after the first 3 cylinders have been discharged. The purpose of the second 3 cylinders is to provide protec-

TM 9-721
42   HEAVY TANKS M6 AND M6A1

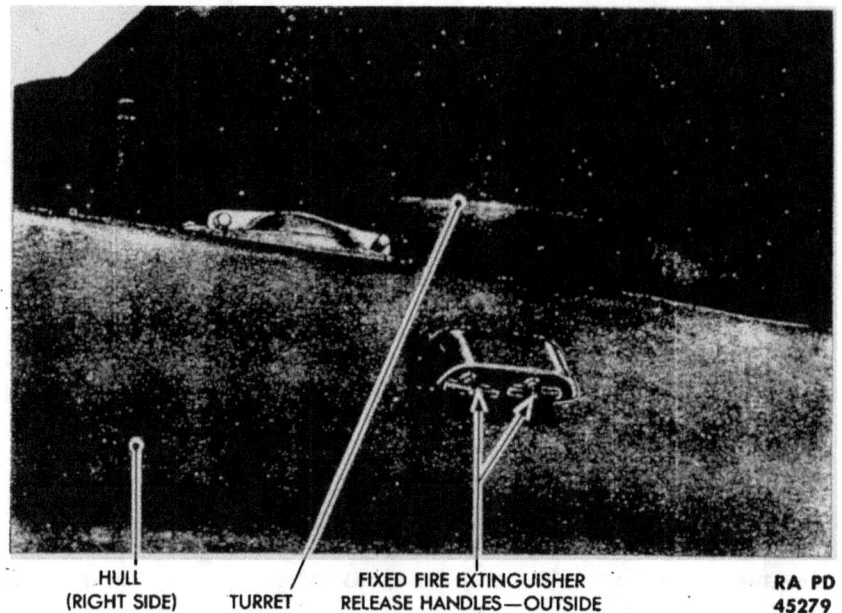

HULL   FIXED FIRE EXTINGUISHER   RA PD
(RIGHT SIDE)   TURRET   RELEASE HANDLES—OUTSIDE   45279

Figure 14—Location of Fixed Fire Extinguisher Outside Release Handles

tion in case of second fire after the first 3 cylinders have been discharged.

c. Principle.

(1) The fire extinguishing system uses carbon dioxide as the extinguishing agent. Carbon dioxide (not to be confused with carbon monoxide) is not poisonous, but is suffocating.

(2) "Fast" fires, such as those involving gasoline or oil, are quickly extinguished by flooding the area with carbon dioxide gas. This reduces the oxygen content and creates an inert atmosphere which smothers the fire. "Slow" or "deep-seated" fires, such as fires in baled cotton and similar substances, are extinguished by prolonged action of a high concentration of carbon dioxide. In addition to its smothering action, carbon dioxide is aided in extinguishing fires by its cooling effect.

(3) Since a person cannot breathe, but will suffocate in an atmosphere of carbon dioxide, caution must be taken before entering any space filled with this gas. Thoroughly ventilate the space into which the gas has been discharged to make certain that all portions contain only fresh air. Should it be necessary for a person to enter a space before it is thoroughly ventilated, he may do so for a short period by holding his breath.

(4) Should a person be overcome by carbon dioxide, it is essential that

TOOLS AND EQUIPMENT

he be rescued from the space containing the gas within 5 minutes. To revive a person so overcome, give him plenty of fresh air and apply artificial respiration as in the case of drowning.

d. Portable Fire Extinguishers. Portable extinguishers are operated by pulling the trigger while directing the discharge cone toward the fire. The position of the trigger determines the rate of discharge. The extinguisher should be carried in the left hand and the hose or cone in the right. Direct the discharge at the base of the flame, with the cone as close to the flame as the operator can safely hold it. Decrease the rate of discharge from the extinguisher as the fire is put out.

e. Fire Extinguisher Care.

(1) Any cylinder containing gas under high pressure is as dangerous as a loaded shell. The extinguisher cylinders should never be dropped, struck, handled roughly, or exposed to unnecessary heat.

(2) WHEN TO EXCHANGE. After use, the extinguisher should be immediately exchanged for one that is fully charged. Every 4 months, or preferably more often, weigh each extinguisher. If the extinguisher weighs less than $3\frac{1}{2}$ pounds (portable) or $9\frac{1}{2}$ pounds (fixed) it should be exchanged for a fully charged one.

(3) CHECK SECURITY. Care should be taken to see that extinguishers are always securely fastened inside the vehicle, and that other equipment does not interfere with the accessibility of controls or ease of operation of the fixed fire extinguisher system.

(4) PERIODIC INSPECTION. The fire extinguishing system requires no more than ordinary care to insure its proper operation. As the system is for emergency use, it must be kept in operating condition at all times; therefore, frequent inspection should be made to insure that apparatus is intact. Check red cap on safety outlet of valve. If not intact, cylinder has been prematurely discharged due to high temperature and must be recharged immediately. The following inspections will be performed:

(a) Daily. Inspect entire system for any mechanical damage. Make certain that shielded nozzles are free of all foreign matter.

(b) Fifty-hour Inspection. Weigh cylinders to determine the carbon dioxide content. Do not attempt to determine content by means of a pressure gage. Empty weight and carbon dioxide charge are stamped on cylinder valve body. Proceed as follows:

1. Remove cylinders.

2. Weigh cylinders and subtract from this weight the empty weight that is stamped on valve body. Empty weight includes cylinder valve and cylinder, but does not include the control head. If the resulting net weight of either cylinder has decreased to below 9 pounds, cylinder must be recharged to its full rated capacity of 10 pounds.

3. Install cylinders.

Section XII

ORGANIZATION SPARE PARTS AND ACCESSORIES

	Paragraph
Organization spare parts and accessories	43

43. ORGANIZATION SPARE PARTS AND ACCESSORIES.

a. A set of organization spare parts and accessories is supplied to the using arms for field replacement of those parts most likely to become broken, worn, or otherwise unserviceable. The set is kept complete by requisitioning new parts for those used. Organization spare parts are listed in pertinent standard nomenclature lists.

b. Care of organization spare parts and accessories is covered in section VI.

TM 9-721
44

Section XIII

ENGINE AND ACCESSORIES

	Paragraph
General description	44
Periodic inspection (50-hour)	45
Periodic inspection (100-hour)	46
Trouble shooting	47
Removal of engine	48
Installation of engine	49

44. GENERAL DESCRIPTION (figs. 15, 16 and 17).

a. General. The Wright Cyclone engine is of the single row, 9 cylinder, air-cooled, static radial type, operating on the conventional 4-stroke cycle. The cylinder bore is 6.125 inch (155.6 mm), and the piston stroke is 6.875 inch (174.6 mm), giving a total piston displacement of 1,823 cubic inches (29.88 liters).

b. Use of Nomenclature. Throughout this book the flywheel end of the engine will be referred to as the "drive-end," and the antiflywheel end will be referred to as the "accessory-end." The terms "right" and "left" refer to the sides of the engine as viewed from the accessory-end. Rotation of the crankshaft is clockwise as viewed from this position. Horizontal and vertical positions of the engine will be referred to with respect to the position of the crankshaft. The cylinders are numbered in a clockwise direction, the top cylinder being number one. Following this designation, the firing order is 1, 3, 5, 7, 9, 2, 4, 6, 8. The right magneto fires the drive-end spark plugs and the left magneto fires the accessory-end spark plugs.

c. Cylinders. Each cylinder is built up by screwing and shrinking a cast aluminum head onto a forged steel barrel. The rocker support boxes are cast integrally with the head. The head is finned for cooling, the fins being a part of the casting. The exhaust port faces to the right side and the intake port to the rear of the cylinder. Bronze valve guides are shrunk into bosses within the valve ports. Valve seat inserts are shrunk into the inside of the head.

d. Crankcase. The crankcase is composed of three aluminum alloy castings, secured together with studs through substantial flanges. The three sections are referred to as the front section, front main section, and rear main section.

e. Crankshaft. The crankshaft is a two-piece, single-throw counterbalanced assembly. The front section of the shaft consists of the shaft proper, the front crankcheek with its counterweight, and the crankpin. The rear section of the shaft consists of the rear crankcheek with its counterweight and the rear main bearing journal. The dynamic damper

77

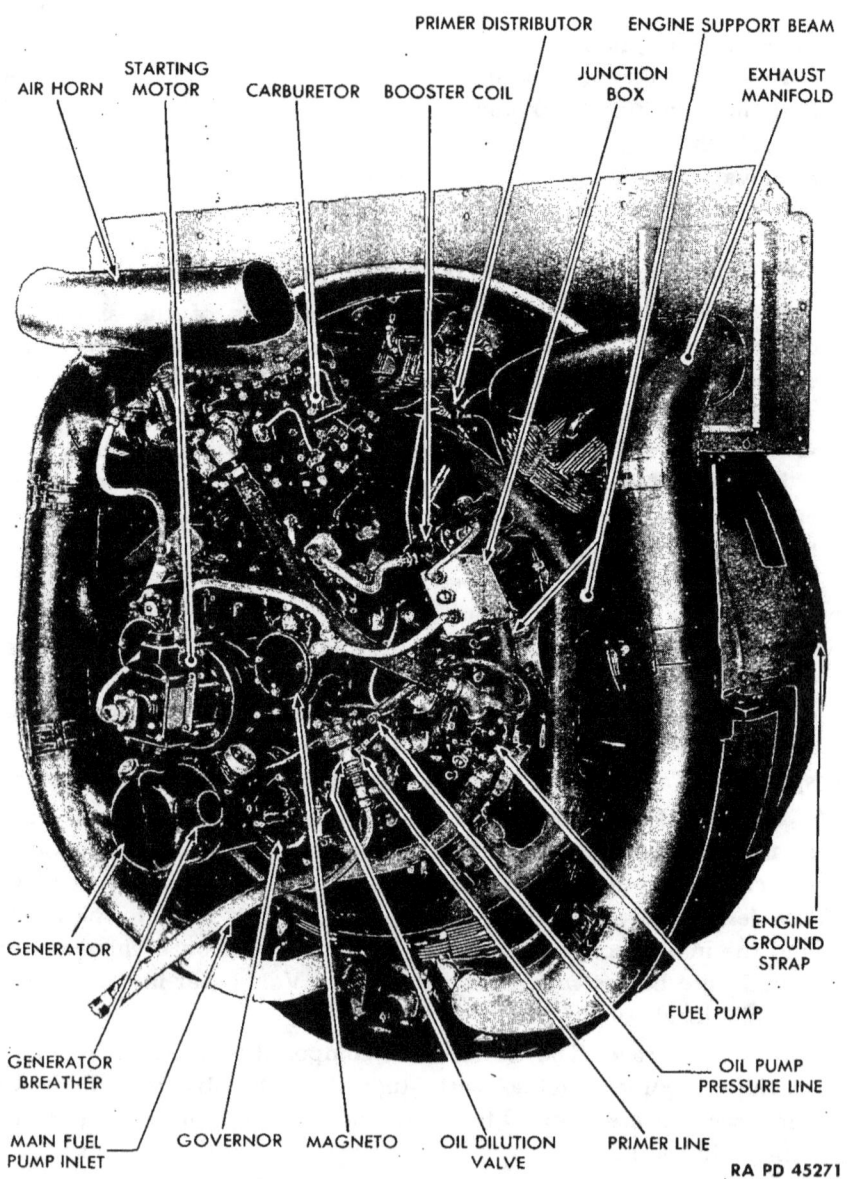

Figure 15 — Right Side View of Engine — Accessory-end

ENGINE AND ACCESSORIES

TM 9-721
44

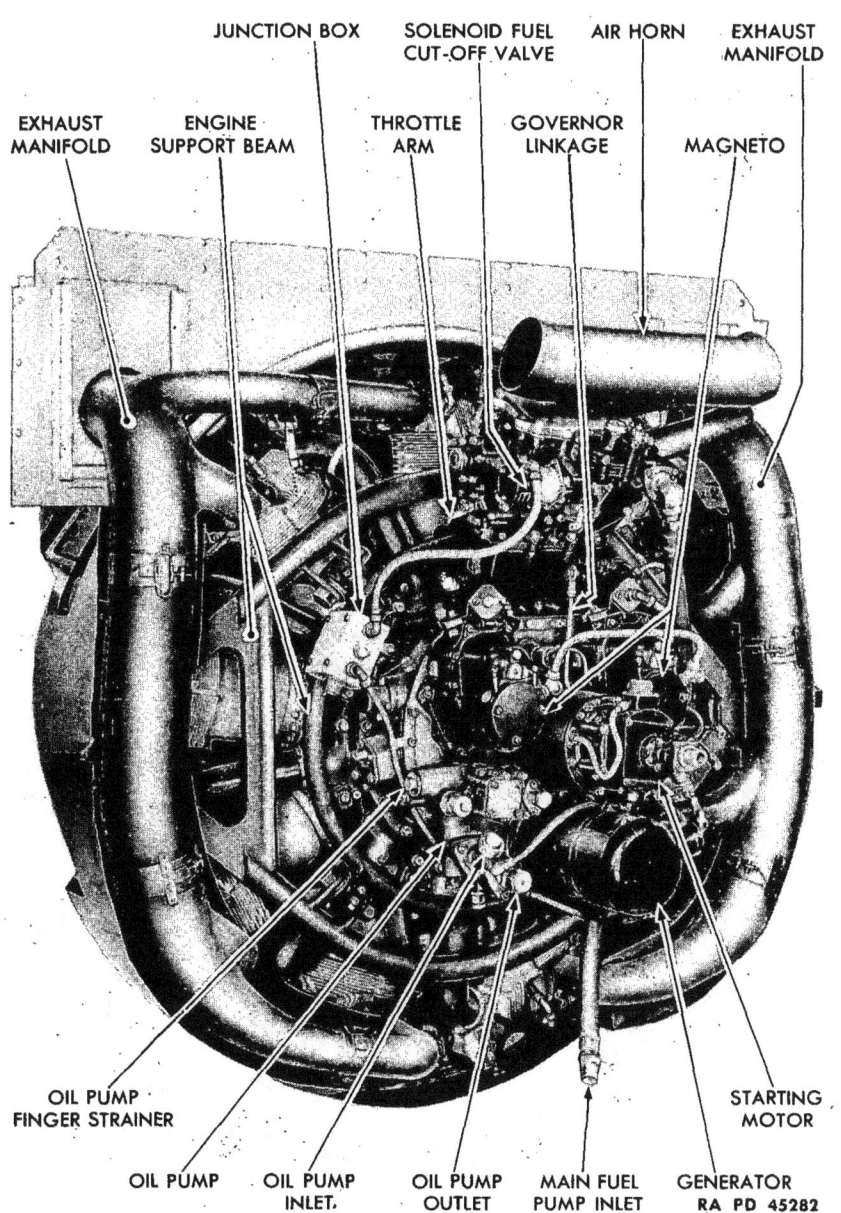

Figure 16—Left Side View of Engine—Accessory-end

TM 9-721
HEAVY TANKS M6 AND M6A1

consists of a steel counterweight, similar in shape to that of the conventional counterweight, hung on an extension of the rear crankcheek by two loose-fitting pins.

f. Master and Connecting Rods. The connecting rod assembly consists of the master rod and articulated connecting rods. The master rod is of one-piece construction and operates in No. 1 cylinder.

g. Pistons. The aluminum alloy forged pistons are of the full-trunk type. There are five piston ring grooves in each piston.

Figure 17 — Drive-end View of Engine

ENGINE AND ACCESSORIES

h. Valve Operating Mechanism. A circular cam, riding on a steel sleeve, which is screwed onto the crankshaft rear main bearing extension, actuates the intake and exhaust valves through cam followers, push rods and rocker arms.

i. Accessories. The two magnetos, starter, generator, governor, oil pump and fuel pump are mounted on the supercharger rear housing cover at accessory-end of the engine. The carburetor is mounted on the extreme upper end of the supercharger rear housing. The supercharger rear housing is attached to the supercharger front housing, and encloses the gear train which drives the various accessories.

j. Engine Supports. The engine is supported in the engine compartment by a "banjo" support beam at the accessory-end, and by support brackets at the drive-end (fig. 16).

k. Data.

(1) GENERAL.

Make and model	Wright G-200
Type	Single row, radial
Number of cylinders	9
Bore	6.125 in.
Stroke	6.875 in.
Piston displacement	1,823 cu in.
Compression ratio	4.92:1
Supercharger impeller diameter	11.00 in.
Supercharger gear ratio	7.0:1
Rated horsepower and rpm	800/2,300 rpm

Cylinder temperatures—(maximum)	Heads	Barrels
Normal rated power—continuous operation	425 F	300 F
Normal rated power to 90% rated power—1-hr operation	450 F	300 F
70% normal rated power	400 F	275 F

Oil pressure lb/sq in.	65 to 75
Oil inlet temperature—(desired)	160 F-180 F
(maximum)	200 F
Fuel pressure lb/sq in.	15 to 18
Rotation of crankshaft (viewed from accessory-end)	Clockwise
Drive shaft to crankshaft ratio	Direct drive
Drive shaft size	SAE No. 40 spline
Average weight of engine	1,350 lb
Over-all length of engine	51.93 in.
Diameter of mounting bolt circle	23.375 in.
Mounting bolts (9)	0.438 in.
Over-all diameter of engine (over rocker box cover studs)	55.07 in.

HEAVY TANKS M6 AND M6A1

(2) IGNITION.

Magneto type	Scintilla SF9LN-5
Spark plugs, types	BG-LS465
	Champion 34-S
	AC-LS87
Spark plug gap	0.012 in.

Magneto timing:
Engine setting	Set No. 1 cylinder at 10° B.T.C. on compression stroke
Right magneto setting	Fixed set at 10° B.T.C.
Left magneto setting	Fixed set at 10° B.T.C.

(3) VALVES AND TIMING.

Intake opens, degrees B.T.C.	5°
Intake closes, degrees A.B.C.	27°
Exhaust closes, degrees B.B.C.	70°
Exhaust closes	T.D.C.
Intake valve remains open, crankshaft degrees	212°
Exhaust valves remain open, crankshaft degrees	250°
Valve rocker clearance, cold	0.010 in.
Timing clearance	0.075 in.
Running clearance	0.075 in.

(4) FUEL SYSTEM.

Carburetor type	Ceco-1900-CPB2
Fuel specification, octane	W. A. C. specification No. 5832
	U. S. Army specification No. 2-103

(5) LUBRICATION SYSTEM.

Oil specification, grade	W. A. C. specification No. 5817

Oil consumption:
Normal rated power and speed	0.025 lb/BHP/hr
70% normal rated power and 89% normal rated speed	0.020 lb/BHP/hr
Cuno oil strainer	Automatic

Tachometer drive ratio:
Mechanical	0.5:1
Electrical	0.5:1

45. PERIODIC INSPECTION (50-HOUR).

a. Periodic inspections given in full in paragraph 20, section IV, included inspections applying to the engine. These inspections have been grouped together for convenient reference and must be made regularly and completely. Periodic inspection, with proper adjustments or repairs being made immediately, is the surest way to protect the life and efficiency of the engine.

46. PERIODIC INSPECTION (100-HOUR).

a. It is important at this time to inspect all lines for signs of leaks before the engine has been cleaned, since evidence of leakage may be entirely removed by cleaning. Spark plugs are not to be removed until after engine has been cleaned. Replace old plugs with dummy plugs to keep all dirt out of the engine interior until new plugs can be installed. Take particular care in disconnecting and connecting all lines and leads to avoid the necessity of replacement because of damage directly due to removal or installation of engine.

47. TROUBLE SHOOTING.

a. This paragraph is devoted to a discussion of the most common engine troubles and their likely causes. Its purpose is to minimize, insofar as possible, the time wasted in locating the source of a given trouble.

b. General Trouble Shooting Procedure. The best method of trouble shooting is to consider all possible causes and eliminate them, one by one, starting with the *most* probable cause. First, determine in what system the trouble exists, whether it is in the fuel system, electrical system, or lubrication system. Then check that particular system, beginning at the source. Thus, in case of trouble in the electrical system battery circuit, the battery would be the first point to check. Similarly, the fuel supply would be checked first if trouble were localized in fuel system.

c. Localizing Troubles. Make an attempt to further localize and isolate troubles by classifying them as general troubles and local troubles. A general trouble is one affecting all cylinders alike, in which case the mechanic will know that the difficulty must be in some accessory that will affect all cylinders. For example, if all cylinders fail to fire, it is likely that magnetos, rather than all nine spark plugs, are at fault. However, if only one cylinder is missing, it can be assumed that magnetos are not at fault, since, if they will fire eight cylinders, they should fire the ninth. This will localize the trouble to spark plugs or spark plug leads of that particular cylinder.

d. Reporting Major Troubles. While the following material (engine troubles and their remedies) will help to locate and correct many engine conditions which may arise in the field, the engine *is not to be experimented on*. If the source of trouble cannot be readily located, or if there is any doubt as to the correct remedy, report the trouble immediately to the proper authority.

e. Engine Fails to Start. If engine fails to start after repeated attempts, the trouble may be in the fuel system, ignition system, mechanical, or a combination. If the priming pump is delivering a charge (which can be determined by feel), the priming system can be used to determine if the ignition system is operative. With the engine receiving a priming charge, there should be firing in a few cylinders until the charge is exhausted. If there is *no* evidence of firing in any cylinder, it can be assumed that the ignition system is at fault. Coughing or sputtering, with failure to start, indicates failure in the fuel system.

f. Engine Starts but Stops. It may be assumed that if the ignition system will fire the engine for a minute or so, it will operate it indefinitely. If engine stops with sputtering and backfiring, the trouble probably lies in the carburetor or fuel system. If engine stops abruptly, as when switching from a good to a defective magneto, the fault will likely be found in the ignition system.

g. Engine Runs but Does not Stop. Proper stopping of the engine is done by operating the solenoid fuel cut-off valve by means of the toggle switch on instrument panel. If engine fails to stop with toggle switch held in "ON" position, the fault must lie in solenoid operation or linkage. If solenoid is inoperative, the fault is either in the wiring to instrument panel, or within the solenoid. Loose linkage will permit the solenoid to operate without affecting the valve. Tighten sufficiently to correct the condition, but not enough to interfere with free return of the valve to the closed position.

h. Low Power and Uneven Running. If engine runs unevenly, determine whether it does so on one or both magnetos. If it runs unevenly on both magnetos, a system other than ignition is probably at fault. If irregularity occurs on only one magneto, that magneto or its attached wires and spark plugs must be the cause.

i. Carburetor Air Cleaners. Although the carburetor air cleaners will handle very heavy concentrations of dust, the cleaners will not function properly if the oil in the oil reservoir is allowed to become too thick with dust to wash the filter element properly. Service the cleaner frequently. To service air cleaners, remove the oil reservoirs from the air cleaner housings. Empty dirt and oil from the reservoir and fill with a light grade of engine oil. An SAE 10 for cold weather or SAE 30 in summer is recommended. Other than selecting an oil that will not evaporate, the quality is unimportant. Heavy or dirty oils will not effectively wash the dust from the filter element. Heavy oils diluted with solvents should not be used, since the solvents evaporate very quickly. The filter elements, being self-washing, should require no attention if the oil in the cups is kept reasonably clean. However, inspect the filters occasionally and wash in solvents if they should appear to be clogging. An air cleaner can clean only the air passing through it. The air connections between the air cleaner and engine must be kept airtight. Small leaks no larger than a pinhole will allow a surprising amount of dust to pass through.

ENGINE AND ACCESSORIES

TM 9-721
47

j. Carburetor Leakage.

(1) Because of the fire hazard, the engine should not be run if the carburetor leaks gasoline. The leakage may be caused by:

(a) Leaky or stuck float.

(b) Excessive fuel supply pressure.

(c) Poor seating of the needle valve.

(d) Wear of the float fulcrum pin.

(e) Improper float level.

(2) In any case, the carburetor should be removed and checked.

k. Spark Plugs. When a spark plug is removed from an engine, due to suspected trouble, it should be inspected thoroughly before disassembly. If the electrodes are heavily coated with carbon, the compression of the cylinder should be checked to determine whether the piston rings are worn or stuck, and therefore allowing oil to pass. A coating of fresh oil also indicates that the spark plug may not have been firing. Check the intake pipes for possible oil leakage past the impeller shaft oil seal. If the spark plug electrodes are free from carbon but discolored, and if they appear to have been running hot, detonation from a poor grade of fuel, or operating under excessive loads, may have been the cause. If the electrodes are coated with a white powder, after operating with tetraethyl lead fuel, the plug may not have been firing and may have been overheated. The spark plug gap should be checked. The core should be inspected for tightness, and the ignition wire and terminals should be inspected for failure. If the plug is disassembled, the core should be inspected for defects in the mica insulation. The plug should be replaced if the insulation is found to be broken, flaked, or dented, or if any mica laminations project beyond adjacent laminations.

l. Magnetos. Trouble with burned magneto points may be traced in some instances to the application of excessive quantities of oil. If excessive oil has been applied, the magneto breaker assembly should be thoroughly cleaned and the points reset. In order to prevent faulty operation of the magnetos during conditions of high humidity, it is recommended that the dielectric parts be treated against moisture absorption. Particular attention should be paid to the distributor block, distributor cylinder, booster and coil terminal blocks, booster collector ring, condenser, and coil. If the dielectric parts have previously been treated with lacquer and if the lacquer is in good condition, merely wipe the parts carefully with a clean cloth. When the lacquer is flaked or in otherwise poor condition, magnetos should be removed and overhauled by proper personnel. For dielectric parts that have been treated with oil, wipe the parts with a clean cloth and then rub them for a few minutes with a cloth moistened with OIL, lubricating, engine, SAE 40.

m. Trouble Shooting.

(1) ENGINE FAILS TO START.

Probable Cause	Probable Remedy
Lack of fuel.	Check fuel supply. Check position and operation of shut-off valves (figs. 24 and 25). Check fuel lines and operation of fuel pump. Remove, inspect, and clean carburetor inlet screen.
Incorrect throttle opening.	Check position of hand throttle. Set to not more than one-tenth open while attempting to start engine.
Water in carburetor.	Remove drain plug. Drain off fuel and water.
Overpriming.	Turn engine over with starting motor, with ignition switch "ON" and throttle at full open position.
Underpriming.	Prime according to instructions (par. 9 b).
Raw fuel in air scoop.	Remove the air scoop from the carburetor. If this is found to be partially filled with gasoline, it will be necessary to remove the carburetor in order to check for sticking of the float needle valve. In addition to checking the needle valve, check to insure that the needle valve seat has not been tampered with so as to leave a gap between the lower end of the seat and the seating gasket. If adjustment of float level is necessary, these gaskets may be obtained in various thicknesses from $\frac{1}{64}$ to $\frac{1}{16}$ inch.
Inoperative booster coil.	Check booster output by holding lead $\frac{3}{8}$ inch from ground. Check leads, wiring, and switch. See that booster is grounded to engine.

ENGINE AND ACCESSORIES

Probable Cause	Probable Remedy
Loose, grounded, or broken ignition wiring.	Inspect all connections. Test lines for breaks or grounds with test light.
Inoperative spark plugs.	Clean gap or replace plugs.
Defective battery.	Recharge or replace battery.
Faulty magneto breaker points.	Check for presence of oil, pitting, or dirt. Check gap and adjust to 0.012 inch. Test spark with electric tester.
Incorrect valve clearance.	Check valve clearance (engine must be removed from tank).
Incorrect valve timing.	Check valve timing (engine must be removed from tank).

(2) ENGINE STARTS BUT STOPS.

Fuel pump inoperative.	Check fuel pump.

(3) ENGINE FAILS TO STOP.

Fuel shut-off valve inoperative.	Inspect valve.

(4) LOW POWER AND UNEVEN RUNNING, ENGINE ROLLS OR EMITS BLACK SMOKE.

Mixture too rich.	Check setting of mixture control. Check fuel pressure at carburetor end of oil dilution line, using low pressure gage. Replace fuel bypass regulator valve if pressure is too high.

(5) UNEVEN RUNNING, WITH OVERHEATING OR BACKFIRING.

Mixture too lean, low fuel pressure, or low fuel supply.	Check setting of mixture control. Raise fuel pressure at fuel pump. Check all intake pipe connections for leaks. Check intake pipe and carburetor elbow for cracks. Check fuel cut-off linkage for bent rod, too short adjustment or any other condition which would allow fuel cut-off valve to remain partially open. Replenish fuel supply.
Improper fuel.	Drain tanks and refill with proper grade of fuel.
Clogged fuel inlet screen.	Remove and clean fuel inlet screen.

Probable Cause	Probable Remedy
Clogged or restricted fuel lines.	Check lines for kinks or restrictions. If necessary, remove and blow out lines.
Faulty carburetor.	If carburetor leaks or is cracked, replace immediately.
Incorrect governor setting.	Check only. If butterfly valve, as indicated by control arm on throttle box, closes before engine reaches prescribed maximum speed, report condition for correction.

(6) STOPPING OR ABNORMAL DROP IN REVOLUTIONS PER MINUTE WHEN SWITCHING FROM ONE MAGNETO TO THE OTHER.

Probable Cause	Probable Remedy
Faulty magneto.	Check breaker points. Check circuit to magneto switch by removing ground wires at magneto. Check distributor blocks for proper seating. Loose covers may allow blocks to jar out of place. Check secondary circuit.
Faulty spark plugs.	Check plugs.
Faulty ignition wiring.	Remove and check spark plug leads for fraying, breaks, saturation with oil, and condition at terminals. Check leads from distributor blocks. Check ignition harness conduit for severe dents which might ground wires.

(7) ENGINE OVERHEATING.

Probable Cause	Probable Remedy
Faulty fuel system.	Check for lean fuel mixture. Check valve clearance. Check grade of fuel.
Faulty lubrication system.	Check efficiency of oil cooler. Check grade of oil. Check oil supply. Check scavenge pump.
Faulty cooling.	Check engine and engine compartment for presence of dirt, particularly around lower cylinders. Check all air passages for obstructions.

(8) LOSS OF OIL PRESSURE.

Probable Cause	Probable Remedy
Insufficient oil supply.	Check oil level.

ENGINE AND ACCESSORIES

Probable Cause	Probable Remedy
Wrong grade of oil.	Drain oil tank and fill with prescribed grade of oil.
Faulty oil pump operation.	Check all oil line connections for air leaks. Also inspect connection at finger strainer in oil pump. Check oil pump operation. Remove oil pressure relief assembly, and check seat of the ball check valve for sticking or improper seating. CAUTION: Be extremely careful to keep all dirt from oil pressure relief assembly when it is removed. Presence of even a minute particle of dust will affect operation of oil pressure relief.
Dirty sump screen.	Remove sump screen and inspect for dirt, particles of metal, and other matter likely to clog screen. NOTE: Presence of metal indicates worn bearings. Report this condition to the proper authority. Check oil filter for presence of metal particles. If any are found, report condition to proper authority.
Sticking oil dilution valve.	Check proper operation of valve by disconnecting fuel line running to dilution valve. Operate switch on instrument panel (fig. 7). This will show if valve is completely closed when the switch is in "OFF" position.
Foam in oil system.	Check for presence of foam by removing oil tank filler pipe cap while the engine is running. The presence of air in the scavenged oil is normal, but in order to eliminate excessive foaming, the return oil from the engine should be directed into the supply tank in such a

Probable Cause	Probable Remedy
Foam in oil system (cont'd.)	manner as to produce a minimum of splashing, and to permit air in the return line to separate from the oil as readily as possible. Oil foaming may also result from cleaning fluid left in tank when flushed. Drain and clean tank and fill with clean oil.
Improper bearing clearance.	Check for presence of metal particles in sump strainer and on magnetic sump drain plug. Report condition to proper authority.
High oil temperature.	Check oil coolers.
Cold-thickened oil.	Evidence — Oil pressure drops when engine speed is increased beyond warm-up speed, due to inability of pump to draw thick oil through lines fast enough. Drop back to warm-up speed until oil reaches higher temperature. See paragraph 32 for special cold weather starting and operating precautions.
Fluctuating oil pressures.	Watch gage for any sudden drop in oil pressure without change in engine speed. NOTE: Oil pressures will normally vary over a considerable range due to changes in engine speed and oil temperature.

(9) HIGH OIL CONSUMPTION.

Probable Cause	Probable Remedy
Faulty oil.	Check for proper grade of oil. Check for oil dilution and inspect operation of oil dilution valve. Check for dirt and sludge.
Insufficient oil supply.	Check oil level in oil tank.
High oil temperature.	Check for air circulation around engine (par. 55).

ENGINE AND ACCESSORIES

Probable Cause	Probable Remedy
Clogged sump strainer.	Remove drain plug and strainer from sump. Clean strainer.
Worn piston rings or cylinders.	Check each cylinder for compression after checking proper valve operation. Report condition to proper authority.
Insufficient air cooling.	Oil tank and lines may be so located that they do not receive the air flow they should. Check the cowling to ascertain that cylinders are receiving sufficient cooling, particularly cylinder barrels. Check for an accumulation of sludge or other foreign material in the external oil system. If the trouble is not located after an investigation of the foregoing, it may be necessary to dismantle the engine to determine whether or not a bearing is overheating or whether any bearing clearance is excessive, causing oil scavenging difficulties. Report condition to proper authority.

48. REMOVAL OF ENGINE.

a. Preliminary Preparation.

(1) Open main battery switch and engine electrical switch on the instrument panel (fig. 7).

(2) Close the four fuel tank shut-off valves and the main fuel shut-off valve (figs. 24, 25 and 39).

(3) Drain oil tank by removing drain plug beneath oil tank.

(4) Remove engine compartment door in front engine compartment bulkhead (fig. 39).

b. Remove Engine Compartment Top Plate and Guard (fig. 4).

(1) Remove pioneer tools and other equipment located on engine compartment top plate and guard.

(2) Remove retaining cap screws which secure engine compartment top plate and guard to hull. Attach cable sling to the top plate. Hook a hoist to the sling and lift off engine compartment top plate.

TM 9-721
48   HEAVY TANKS M6 AND M6A1

(3) Attach a cable sling to the engine compartment guard. Hook a hoist to the sling and remove the engine compartment guard.

c. Remove Mufflers (fig. 18).

(1) Remove clamp screw which secures bracket clamp around muffler (front and rear).

(2) Rotate upper half of bracket clamps up away from muffler.

(3) Loosen the V-clamp which clamps the forward end of the muffler to the exhaust tube.

(4) Lift out muffler with attached tail pipe.

(5) Work the exhaust tube free from the exhaust manifold, then pull out the exhaust tube.

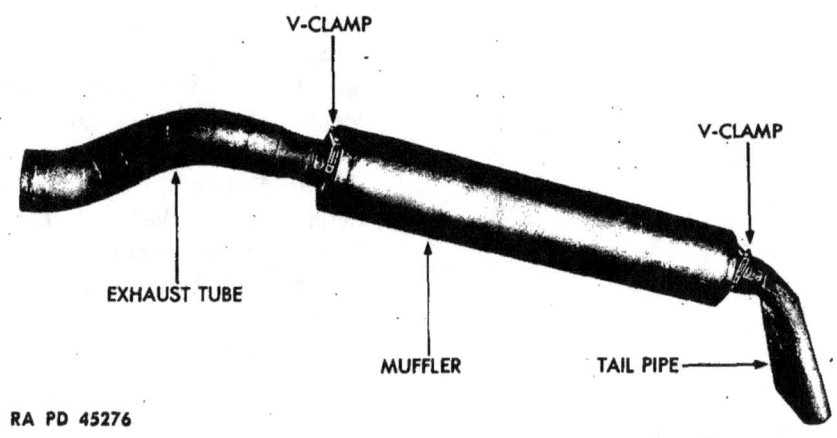

RA PD 45276

Figure 18 — Exhaust Tube, Muffler and Tail Pipe Assembly

d. Remove Engine Components which Interfere with the Removal of Engine (figs. 15, 16 and 19). NOTE: In order to remove the engine from the vehicle, it is necessary that the generator, starting motor, carburetor and carburetor air horn be removed from the engine. These project from the engine, and unless removed, will catch the sill of the engine compartment bulkhead when the engine is lifted.

(1) REMOVE STARTING MOTOR (fig. 20).

(a) Remove the knurled nut which secures the starting motor cable conduit to the starting motor. Pull out the plug-type electrical connections from the prong within the shield.

(b) Remove the palnuts from the starting motor retaining studs, then remove the retaining nuts. Lift off the starting motor.

ENGINE AND ACCESSORIES

TM 9-721
48

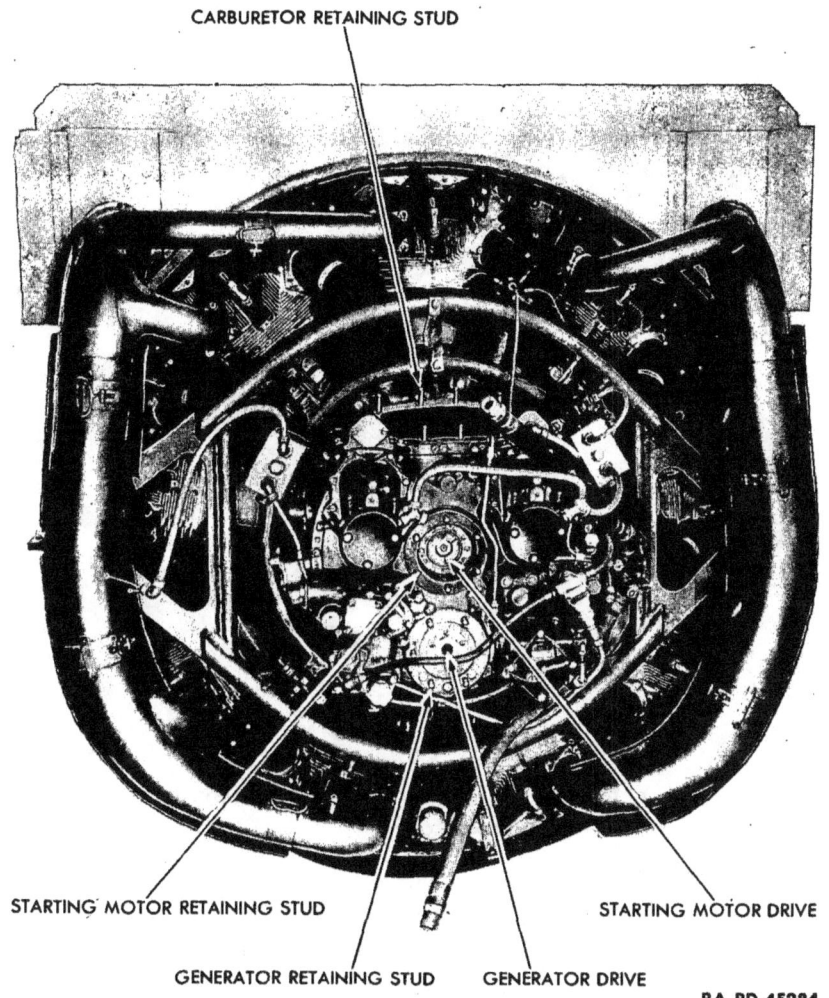

Figure 19 — Accessory-end View of Engine, Carburetor, Starting Motor and Generator Removed

(2) REMOVE GENERATOR (fig. 21).

(a) Remove knurled nut which secures generator cable conduit to generator. Pull out plug-type electrical connection from the prongs within the shield.

(b) Loosen the clamp which secures the generator breather line to the generator. Pull the breather line off the generator breather.

TM 9-721
48
HEAVY TANKS M6 AND M6A1

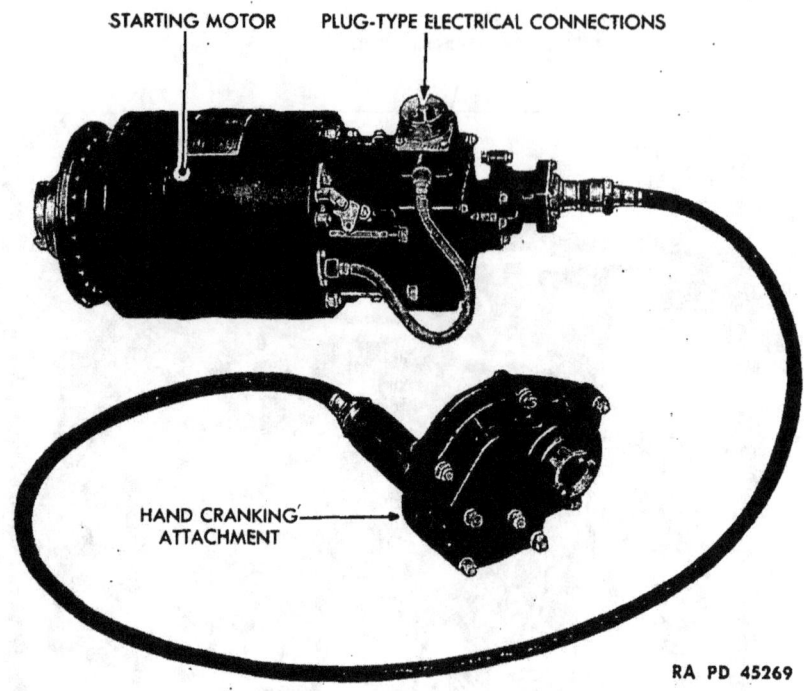

Figure 20 — Starting Motor

(c) Remove generator lock wire or retaining palnuts, then remove retaining nuts. Lift off the generator.

(3) REMOVE CARBURETOR (fig. 19).

(a) Loosen clamp screws which clamp the fabric air intake tubes to the carburetor air horn. Work the fabric tubes off the carburetor air horn.

(b) Remove the safety wire which locks the air horn retaining cap screws. Remove the cap screws and lift off the carburetor air horn.

(c) Disconnect fuel line from the fuel pump to the carburetor, at the carburetor. Plug the line with cloth.

(d) Disconnect the electrical lead from the left junction box to the fuel solenoid cut-off valve on the carburetor.

(e) Disconnect the carburetor accelerator linkage and governor control linkage.

(f) Remove the palnuts which lock the carburetor retaining nuts at the carburetor throttle box. Remove the retaining nuts which secure the carburetor throttle box, and lift off the carburetor.

ENGINE AND ACCESSORIES

TM 9-721
48

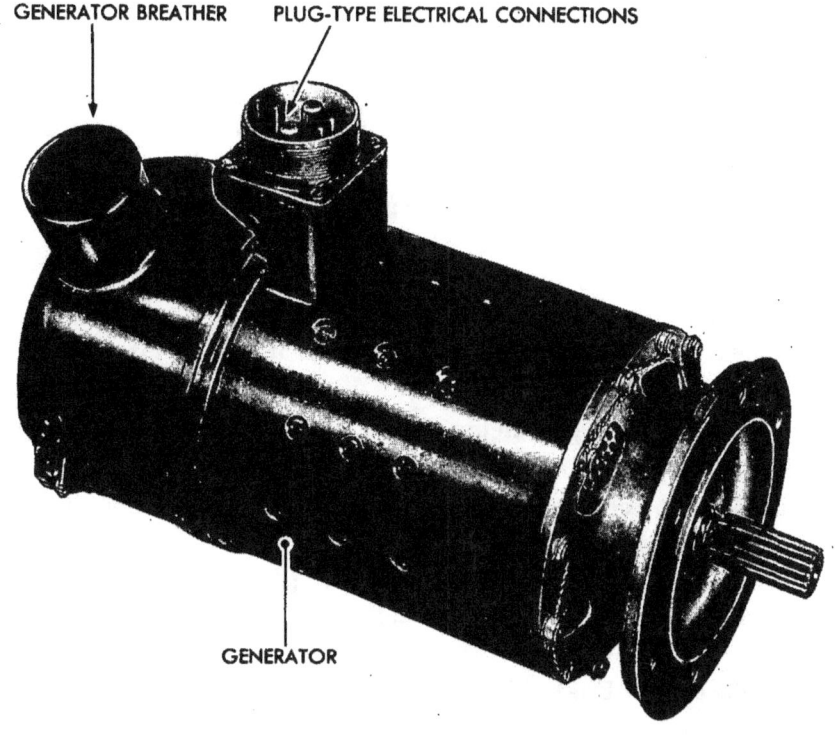

Figure 21 — Generator

(g) Install metal or cardboard plate of some type over the throttle box opening on the engine to prevent foreign materials from dropping into the engine.

e. Remove Engine Compartment Shrouds.

(1) Disconnect and remove the rear engine compartment shroud.

(2) Disconnect front engine compartment shroud at hull. **NOTE:** Do not attempt to disconnect the front engine compartment shroud at the engine. It is left in place on the engine and removed from the vehicle with the engine.

f. Disconnect Primer Line (fig. 15). Disconnect primer line from primer pump to primer distributor, at flexible hose in front of the front fire extinguisher nozzle.

g. Disconnect Oil Pump Pressure Line (fig. 15). Disconnect the oil pump pressure line at the flexible hose next to the primer line. Plug open lines with cloth.

h. Disconnect Oil Temperature Line. Disconnect the oil temperature gage line from bottom of oil pump.

i. Disconnect Oil Inlet and Oil Outlet Lines (fig. 16). Disconnect the oil pump inlet and outlet lines at the oil pump. Plug open ends of lines and oil pump with cloth after disconnecting the lines.

j. Disconnect the Engine Breather Line. Disconnect the engine breather line from the rear supercharger housing line just above the starting motor.

k. Disconnect Main Fuel Inlet Line (fig. 15). Disconnect the fuel inlet line from the fuel filter to the fuel pump, at the fuel filter. Plug open end of line with cloth.

l. Disconnect Tachometer Shaft. Unscrew tachometer conduit knurled nut. Slip out tachometer splined shaft.

m. Disconnect Engine Ground Strap (fig. 15). Disconnect the engine ground strap.

n. Disconnect Engine Support Beam (fig. 15). Remove the two nuts and bolts which secure each side of the engine support beam to brackets on the hull.

o. Disconnect Engine Support Brackets.

(1) Remove the cover from the box which surrounds the engine support brackets at the rear of the engine (each side of the engine).

(2) Remove the nuts and bolts which secure the engine support brackets to the brackets on the hull.

p. Attach Engine Lifting Sling (fig. 22). Lay the engine lifting sling on top the engine. The two hooked cables pass down the accessory-end of the engine and hook on each side of the engine support beam. The curved bar on the opposite end of the sling hooks onto the flange of the engine flywheel.

q. Remove Engine from Vehicle. Attach a hoist to the engine lifting sling. Carefully lift the engine from the vehicle. *Take extreme care to see that no part of the engine catches on any projecting part in the engine compartment.* When the engine is clear of the vehicle, lower to stand previously prepared. Remove engine lifting sling.

49. INSTALLATION OF ENGINE.

a. Attach Engine Lifting Sling (fig. 22). Lay the engine lifting sling on top of the engine. The two hooked cables pass down the accessory-end of the engine, and hook on each side of the engine support beam.

ENGINE AND ACCESSORIES

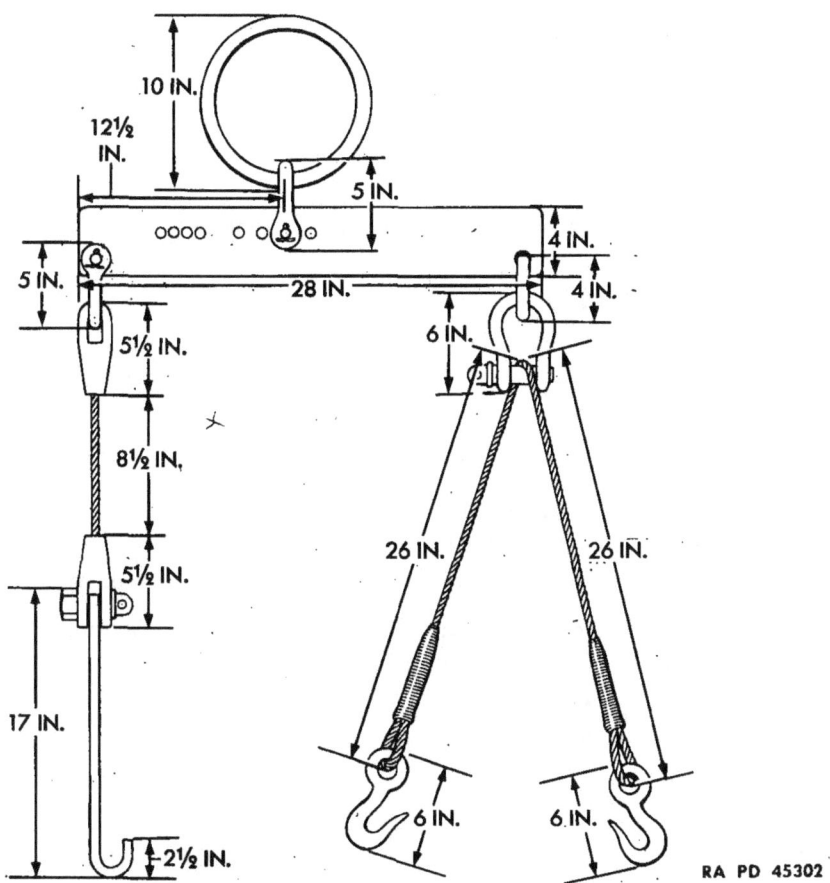

Figure 22 — Detail of Engine Lifting Sling

The curved bar on the opposite end of the sling hooks to the flange of the engine flywheel.

b. Lift Engine into Position. Attach a hoist to the engine lifting sling. Carefully lift the engine up and into position in the vehicle. *Take extreme care to see that no part of the engine catches on any projecting part in the engine compartment.*

c. Connect Engine Support Brackets.

(1) Install the nuts and bolts which secure the engine support brackets to the brackets on the hull.

(2) Install the cover on the box which surrounds the engine support brackets (each side of engine).

d. Connect Engine Support Beam (fig. 15). Install the nuts and bolts which secure each side of the engine support beam to brackets on the hull. Remove lifting sling.

e. Connect Engine Ground Strap (fig. 15). Connect the engine ground strap.

f. Connect Tachometer Shaft. Slide tachometer splined shaft into position. Tighten tachometer conduit knurled nut.

g. Connect Main Fuel Inlet Line (fig. 15).
(1) Remove cloth which plugs open end of line.
(2) Connect the main fuel inlet line from the fuel filter to the fuel pump, at the fuel filter.

h. Connect Engine Breather Line. Connect engine breather line.

i. Connect Oil Inlet and Oil Outlet Lines (fig. 16).
(1) Remove cloth plugs from open lines.
(2) Connect the oil pump inlet and outlet lines at the oil pump.

j. Connect Oil Temperature Line. Connect the oil temperature gage line to the bottom of the oil pump.

k. Connect Oil Pump Pressure Line (fig. 15).
(1) Remove cloth plugs at end of line.
(2) Connect the oil pump pressure line to the flexible hose next to the primer line.

l. Connect Primer Line (fig. 15). Connect primer line from primer pump to primer distributor, at flexible hose directly in front of the front fire extinguisher nozzle.

m. Install and Connect Engine Compartment Shrouds.
(1) Connect the front engine compartment shroud at the hull.
(2) Install and connect the rear engine compartment shroud.

n. Install Engine Components (figs. 19, 20 and 21). Install engine components which were removed to permit installation of engine. NOTE: In order to install the engine in the vehicle it was necessary to remove generator, starting motor, carburetor, and carburetor air horn from the engine. These components may now be installed.

(1) INSTALL STARTING MOTOR (fig. 20).
(a) Place the starting motor in position on the starting motor studs. Install retaining nuts and palnuts.
(b) Plug in the starting motor cable electrical connections. Tighten

ENGINE AND ACCESSORIES

the knurled nut which secures the starting motor cable conduit to the starting motor.

(2) INSTALL GENERATOR (fig. 21).

(a) Place generator in position on generator studs. Install generator retaining nuts and palnuts or lock wire.

(b) Place the generator breather line in position on the generator. Tighten the clamp which secures the breather line.

(c) Plug in generator cable electrical connection. Tighten knurled nut which secures generator cable conduit to generator.

(3) INSTALL CARBURETOR (figs. 15 and 19).

(a) Remove plate which was placed over the throttle box opening on the engine to prevent foreign materials from dropping within the engine.

(b) Place the carburetor on the carburetor studs. Install retaining nuts and palnuts.

(c) Connect carburetor accelerator linkage and governor control linkage.

(d) Connect electrical lead from the left junction box to the fuel solenoid cut-off valve on the carburetor.

(e) Remove cloth plug from fuel line between the fuel pump and carburetor. Connect the line at the carburetor.

(f) Place the carburetor air horn in position. Install retaining cap screws. Lock wire cap screws securely.

(g) Work fabric air intake tubes on the carburetor air horn. Install clamp screws which secure tubes to the air horn.

o. **Install Mufflers** (fig. 18).

(1) Place exhaust tubes (left and right) in position on exhaust manifolds.

(2) Place muffler with attached tail pipe in position. Tighten V-clamp which clamps forward end of muffler to exhaust tube.

(3) Rotate upper half of muffler, bracket clamps into position around muffler. Install bracket clamp screws.

p. **Install Engine Compartment Top Plate and Guard** (fig. 4).

(1) Attach a cable sling to the engine compartment top plate. Hook a hoist to the sling and lift the top plate up and into position on the hull. Install retaining cap screws.

(2) Attach a cable sling to the engine compartment guard. Hook a hoist to the sling and lift the engine compartment guard up and into position on the hull. Install retaining cap screws.

(3) Install pioneer tools and other equipment which were removed to permit the removal of the engine compartment top plate and guard.

q. **Concluding Steps.**

(1) Place engine compartment door in position in front engine compartment bulkhead. Tighten retaining screws (fig. 4).

(2) Install oil tank drain plug. Fill oil tank with proper quantity and grade of oil.

(3) If the vehicle is to be operated immediately, open the four fuel tank shut-off valves and the main fuel shut-off valve (figs. 24, 25 and 39).

(4) Close main battery switch and engine electrical switch on the instrument panel (fig. 7).

Section XIV

FUEL SYSTEM

	Paragraph
Description	50
Inspection	51
Trouble shooting	52
Grades of engine gasoline	53

50. DESCRIPTION.

a. Fuel Tanks. Fuel supply for the Heavy Tanks M6 and M6A1 is carried in four fuel tanks. Fuel tanks are horizontally mounted, two in the left sponson and two in the right sponson. Access to the fuel tanks for filling is provided by fuel filler caps on top the hull (fig. 4). An additional fuel tank containing fuel for the auxiliary generator unit is located in the left sponson ahead of the front left sponson fuel tank, and has a capacity of 6 gallons. Total capacity of all fuel tanks, including the auxiliary generating unit fuel tank, is 483 gallons. Fuel tanks are constructed of fabric and synthetic rubber.

b. Fuel Lines (fig. 23).

(1) From either of the four fuel tanks, fuel goes to a collector or header line. From there it is drawn through the fuel filter and up into the engine fuel pump located on the right side of the engine beneath the right junction box. From the fuel pump it is forced to the carburetor.

(2) A fuel line from the fuel filter connects to the primer pump located on a bracket directly in front of a driver (fig. 6). Upon operation of the pump plunger, fuel drawn in the primer pump is forced back to the priming distributor on the engine, priming the five top cylinders (fig. 15).

(3) An oil dilution valve is fed by a fuel line connecting with the fuel system at the fuel pump outlet to the carburetor (fig. 15). When the valve is open, fuel is allowed to enter the oil inlet line to the engine to dilute the oil in the engine, and to facilitate cold weather starting.

c. Fuel Shut-off Valves (figs. 23, 24 and 25). Five fuel shut-off valves are provided, one for each tank and one main shut-off valve at the fuel filter. Shut-off valves for the left front and left rear tanks project out into the left rear of the driving compartment; those for the right front and right rear tanks project out into the right rear of the driving compartment. The main shut-off valve handle projects through the lower right center of the engine compartment front bulkhead and into the driving compartment. Turn fuel shut-off valve clockwise to shut off the fuel supply.

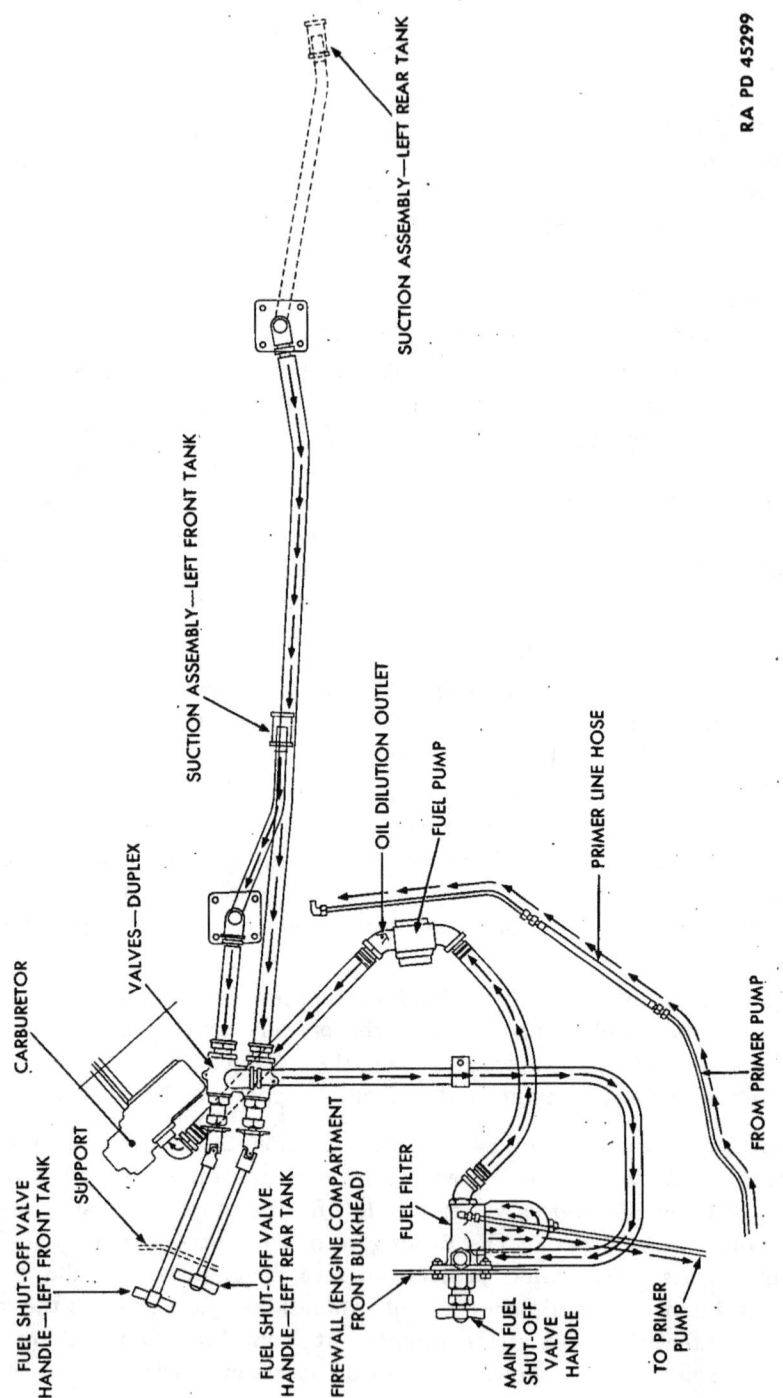

Figure 23—Fuel System

FUEL SYSTEM

TM 9-721
50

Figure 24 — Right Rear Corner of Driving Compartment

Figure 25 — Location of Fuel Shut-off Valve Handles — Right Tank

51. INSPECTION.

a. Inspect all connections and fuel lines periodically for signs of leaks and evidence of damage or wear.

b. Take care to maintain all flexible fuel lines in such a position that they are not subjected to twisting, abrasion, or rubbing against some other line or part.

c. Check the carburetor for signs of leakage. Examine the carburetor closely for cracks.

d. Periodically check all air intake connections for tightness and the presence of even the smallest holes.

52. TROUBLE SHOOTING.

a. Trouble shooting in the fuel system is interrelated with engine trouble shooting which is covered in detail in paragraph 47.

FUEL SYSTEM

53. GRADES OF ENGINE GASOLINE.

a. Commercial gasoline having an octane rating of 80 is preferred, and should be used. Do not use fuel of a rating less than 80. However, engine will operate satisfactorily when fuel with an octane rating as high as 90 is used.

Section XV

COOLING SYSTEM

	Paragraph
Description	54
Inspection and maintenance	55

54. DESCRIPTION.

a. The engine is cooled by an air blast produced by a fan mounted on the engine flywheel (fig. 17). The fan draws air through a guard in the engine compartment front top plate (fig. 4) and forces it between and around the finned cylinders of the engine. The warm air passes out through the rear of the hull. Air ducts are formed on the engine by baffles bolted around and between each cylinder and cylinder head. A shroud forms a further duct for the inlet of air through the guard. A shroud in the engine compartment forces all air drawn in by the fan to pass directly around the engine cylinders.

55. INSPECTION AND MAINTENANCE.

a. At the 100-hour inspection, the cooling fins on the engine cylinders and the surfaces of the shrouding and baffles must be cleaned thoroughly of all accumulated oil and dirt. All bolts on the fan ring, baffles, and fan cowling must be tightened and the fan cowling cleaned. Dirt must be cleaned from the cylinder heads, especially the lower two, at the 50-hour check. Inspect to be sure that stowage on top of the vehicle does not in any way interfere with the free entrance of air into the fan compartment.

Section XVI

TORQUE CONVERTER

	Paragraph
Description	56
Data	57
Inspection	58

56. DESCRIPTION (figs. 10, 26 and 27).

a. The hydraulic torque converter is a form of hydraulic transmission which applies the engine horsepower to the final drive in an infinitely variable torque-speed ratio, wherein the required ratio, within known limitations, is automatically selected solely by the load imposed on the vehicle. The known limitations of torque-speed ratio of the converter require the use of a gear transmission (having two forward speeds and one reverse) between the converter output shaft and the final drive to provide the desired operating range of the vehicle. The converter is mounted directly to this transmission, the transmission input pinion gear being mounted on the converter output shaft. The transmission, in turn, is mounted on the final drive units. Certain maintenance operations, covered in the 50- and 100-hour inspections (pars. 20 and 21) and other inspections (pars. 8, 10, 18 and 19), may be performed while the torque converter is installed in the vehicle. However, for more advanced maintenance, including replacement and repair of the converter, the converter must be removed from the vehicle. This necessitates the removal of the assembled torque converter, transmission, and final drive, since the converter cannot be separated from the transmission until after the entire assembly (fig. 27) has been removed from the vehicle.

b. The converter is directly connected to the engine by means of a flange-type flexible coupling, no clutch being used (fig. 17).

c. Fluid, a distillate type such as No. 1 grade Diesel fuel, is the operating medium of the torque converter, there being no mechanical connection between the input and output ends of the converter.

d. The transmission of power through the converter depends upon the circulatory movement of the fluid within the hydraulic chamber of the converter. This circulatory movement is generated by the converter pump which is driven by the engine at two-thirds engine speed. The pump is of the centrifugal type having 20 blades with a peripheral diameter of approximately 21 inches.

e. The fluid is discharged from the pump into the turbine, passing alternately through three stages of turbine blades and two stages of

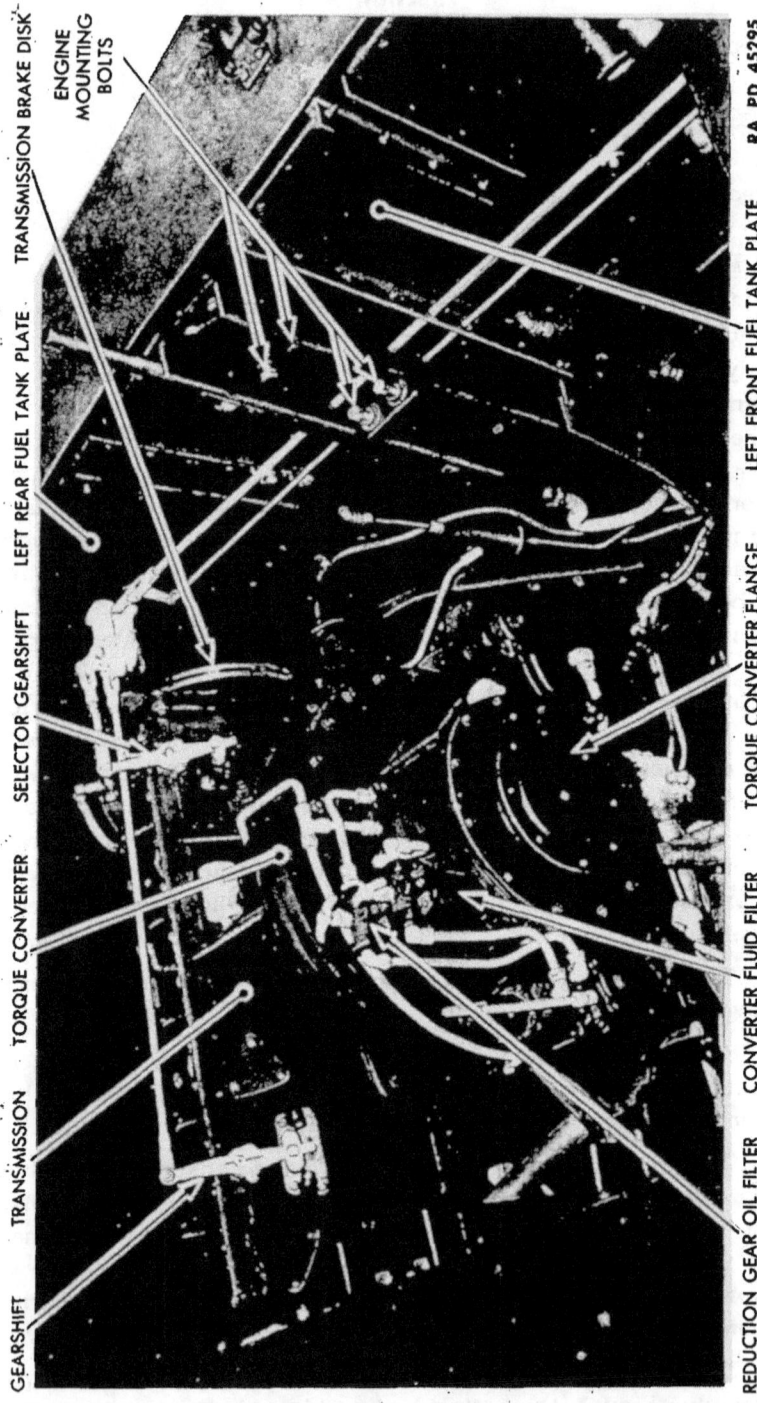

Figure 26 — Installed Torque Converter, Transmission and Final Drive

TORQUE CONVERTER

TM 9-721
56

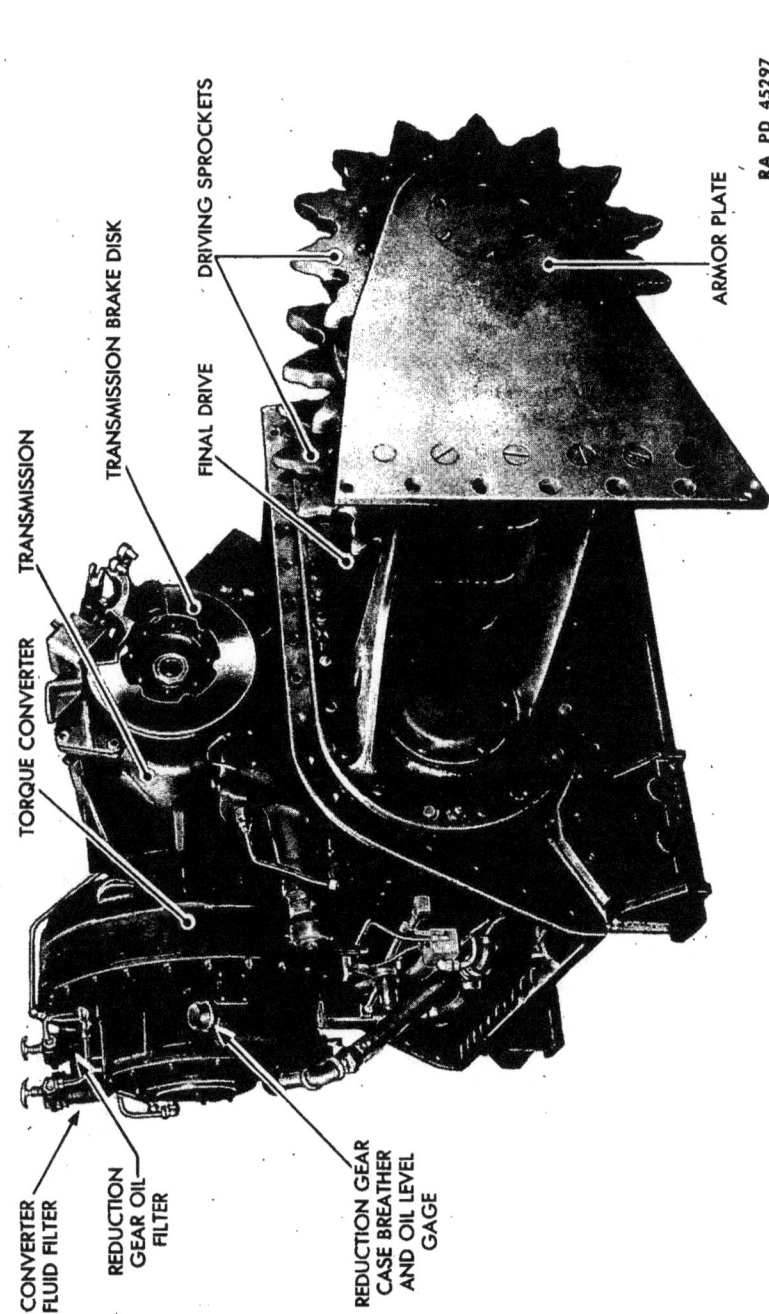

Figure 27 — Torque Converter, Transmission and Final Drive Assembly Removed from Vehicle

reaction blades. As the fluid is exhausted from the third stage turbine blades, it immediately reenters the pump and is recirculated. The turbine is mounted to the converter output shaft through which the power is transmitted to the transmission.

f. Since the torque converter must be completely filled with the proper fluid for satisfactory operation, an expansion tank is provided in the right sponson, to the rear of the air cleaners, to care for the volumetric increase of the fluid as its temperature rises. This tank is provided with an orifice valve which remains open at all times, and through which the expanded fluid escapes from the main fluid circuit. This valve also serves as a continuous vent to relieve the converter of any gas or air that forms or is trapped within the converter. The reserve tank is open to the atmosphere through a breather. A reserve of approximately 2 gallons of fluid is carried in this tank to provide against loss of fluid due to vaporization or small leaks. A bayonet-type gage is provided to check the fluid level. Access to the expansion tank is provided by an armored hinged cap on top of the right sponson, directly above the expansion tank filler cap.

g. A fluid cooler is provided in the left bulkhead for cooling the operating fluid. The outlet from, and the inlet to, the converter, are so arranged that the pressure differential across the converter pump is utilized to circulate the fluid through the cooling radiator, no auxiliary pump being used for this purpose.

h. An auxiliary fluid pump is mounted on the right input side of the converter to insure that the converter remains full of fluid at about 50 pounds per square inch pressure. This prevents cavitation of the fluid around the blades which is detrimental to the efficient operation of the converter. The auxiliary pump also returns to the main circuit that quantity of fluid which is continuously being vented through the orifice valve into the expansion tank.

i. A reduction gear oil pump is also located on the right input side of the converter to provide pressure lubrication to the three-to-two planetary type reduction gear built into the input side of the converter between the input shaft and the converter pump. A reduction gear oil sump of 5-quart capacity is provided in the reduction gear housing.

j. Filters for both the reduction gear oil and the converter fluid are provided on the right input side of the converter adjacent to, and in the pressure discharge lines from, the auxiliary pump assemblies. These filters are provided with handles for daily cleaning of the elements. Access to these filters is through a top deck door.

k. A valve for filling and draining the main fluid circuit of the converter is provided in the 1¼-inch discharge hose from the converter to

TORQUE CONVERTER

the fluid cooler. Access to this valve is through a manhole located in the tank floor on the left side of the engine compartment.

l. Two gages are provided in the instrument panel to indicate temperature and base pressure of the operating fluid (fig. 7).

m. A Hycon pump is located on the right input side of the converter to provide pressure to the Hycon steering brake controls.

57. DATA.

Weight without fluid, radiator, expansion tank and filters	1,330 lb
Length (coupling flange to transmission flange)	20.547 in.
Over-all diameter	30.125 in.

Operating fluid:
    Capacity .... Approx. 35 gal
    Grade .... No. 1 grade Diesel fuel

Lubricating oil (reduction gear):
    Capacity .... 5 qt
    Grade .... 50 SAE, or same used in engine

Operating base pressure (min) .... 50 psi

Operating temperature:
    Normal at 150 F outside air .... 220 F
    Maximum safe continuous duty .... 260 F

58. INSPECTION.

a. Due to the fact that the torque converter constitutes such an important part of the vehicle, most inspections have been included in the inspection section of this manual (sec. IV). In addition to the regular inspections, check lines, fittings and castings frequently for converter fluid or reduction gear oil leaks, and worn or loose parts. Failure to keep lines and fittings tight and in good condition can cause a major failure. Bear in mind that the converter fluid is the main transmission medium.

Section XVII

HYCON SYSTEM

	Paragraph
Description	59
Inspection and maintenance	60
Trouble shooting	61

59. DESCRIPTION.

a. General. The Hycon system of steering and braking controls provides complete hydraulic steering and braking on the Heavy Tanks M6 and M6A1. A Hycon control pedestal placed directly in front of the driver carries two small Hycon steering controls (fig. 6). These are used to steer and brake the vehicle under all normal driving conditions. The full description of the operation on the Hycon controls is given in paragraph 7 b (1). This section will be devoted to a description of more important components which make up the system.

b. Hydraulic Pump. A hydraulic pump is provided to build up the pressure throughout the system.

c. Suction Control Valve. The function of the suction control valve is to close communication between the pump suction line and the sump tank, when pump pressure reaches the predetermined maximum as governed by the adjustment of compression in the control spring. In addition, the suction control valve operates as relief valve to discharge excessive pump pressure directly to the sump tank should a restriction occur in the pump delivery line, or pressure rise more than 300 pounds above normal.

d. Accumulator Sump Tank (fig. 28). The accumulator sump tank is a 10½-inch outside diameter sphere, located in the lower right rear sponson. Access to the tank is provided from within the engine compartment or by removing the protective compartment plate from the right track armor plate. Under operating conditions the center column is filled with hydraulic fluid. The oil in the outer chamber is carried at a predetermined level which fluctuates as oil is withdrawn from or admitted to the pressure tank by operation of the steering and braking controls. This center column is enclosed in a tube, its edges being welded to the pressure tank interior at the top, and having a slight clearance at the bottom. Nitrogen gas under high pressure is admitted to the outside of this column when the tank is initially charged and 2 quarts of glycerin-blend fluid is admitted as an inhibitor of gas and oil diffusion.

e. Automatic Shut-off Valve. The function of the automatic shut-off valve is to prevent exhaustion of the nitrogen gas supply from its chamber

HYCON SYSTEM

TM 9-721
59-60

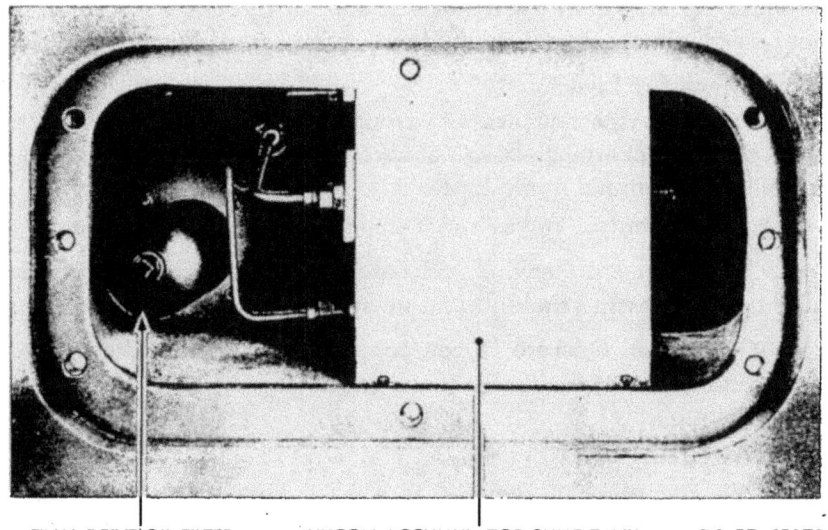

FINAL DRIVE OIL FILTER   HYCON ACCUMULATOR SUMP TANK   RA PD 45278

Figure 28 — Installed Hycon Accumulator Sump Tank and Final Drive Oil Filter

outside the tube inserted in the accumulator, or pressure tank, by limiting the pressure drop in the hydraulic system. If this valve is omitted or functions improperly, continued application of the steering and braking controls when the engine is not running or is idling at too low a speed to maintain the fluid supply at the rate it is exhausted, causes the oil level to fall in the outer chamber of the accumulator tank to a point that nitrogen may escape. Thereafter, the reserve pressure supply, which permits the withdrawal of hydraulic fluid for brake operation for a limited time after the engine stops, will become depleted, and brake operation by hydraulic means will be directly actuated by the pump.

f. **Pressure Control Valve.** It is the function of the pressure control valve to meter hydraulic pressure to the work cylinder line.

g. **Work Cylinder.** The work cylinders, two in number, one right and one left, are the units by which the pressure of the hydraulic system is applied for the actuation of the steering brakes in the controlled differential.

60. INSPECTION AND MAINTENANCE.

a. **General.** In the event of wear or failure of any of the Hycon components, replace the faulty unit. Components which should be replaced as units are work cylinder, control valve, pump, suction control valve, sump tank, accumulator and automatic shut-off valve.

b. Pump. Make sure that all suction line connections are tight. Air drawn in the suction line will make trouble all through the system. Sufficient air leak will prevent the hydraulic pump from functioning.

c. Check for Leaks.

(1) Visibly inspect connections around accumulator, gage connections, work cylinder, charging valve connections, sump tank, suction control and oil fillings around pump for leaks.

(2) Check control valves and T-connections.

d. Pressure. Start engine and note Hycon pressure gage on instrument panel. Pressure should build up steadily to 1,500 pounds.

e. Operation. Operate Hycon controls and note tightness of brake bands, and action of hydraulic boosting.

61. TROUBLE SHOOTING.

a. This paragraph is devoted to a discussion on the most common Hycon troubles, probable causes and probable remedies. Its purpose is to minimize, insofar as possible, the time wasted in locating the source of a given trouble.

(1) HAND CONTROL TRAVEL TOO LONG.

Probable Cause	Probable Remedy
Brake bands loose.	Take up brake bands.

(2) NO PRESSURE.

Probable Cause	Probable Remedy
External leak between accumulator and automatic shut-off valve, or fluid has passed through defective automatic shut-off valve and system lines to sump tank.	Repair leak or renew automatic shut-off valve. Recharge.
Suction control valve improperly set.	These valves are set at factory to cut off flow to pump at 2,000 lb psi and cut in at 1,850 lb psi. If it is desired to lower this, remove cap from the top of the suction control valves. Using spanner wrench, back the screw out to lower pressure (about ½ turn for 50 lb). Replace the cap and tighten. This must hold a vacuum, otherwise instead of pulling oil out of the sump tank, air will be pulled into the system.

HYCON SYSTEM

Probable Cause

Operating engine for long period of time without using steering controls. Suction control valve relieves any additional pressure pumped at 2,300 lb. Heat of engine can cause as much as 400 lb psi variation in pressure tank.

(3) PRESSURE TOO LOW.

Sump tank vent or air filter plugged, preventing oil from reaching pump.

Fluid exhausted from sump tank, or level too low.

Loose connections or loose cap on suction control valve, causing air instead of oil to be drawn to pump.

Suction control valve improperly set.

Probable Remedy

Hycon parts are factory tested at 3,000 lb psi. Pressure can always be reduced by operating steering levers.

Remove vent and clean.

Replenish oil supply using No. 2 Hycon fluid or No. 7, No. 8, or No. 9 refined petroleum oil (clear petroleum oil is preferable if oil in system gives evidence of thickening).

Tighten all connections.

Remove cap from top of suction control valve and, using spanner wrench, tighten the screw to higher pressure (about ½ turn to 50 lb). Replace cap and tighten. **CAUTION**: This valve was set at factory to cut off at approximately 2,000 lb.

Section XVIII

POWER TRAIN

	Paragraph
Description	62
Adjustment of steering and parking brakes	63
Lubrication of transmission and final drive	64

62. DESCRIPTION (fig. 27).

a. General. Power is transmitted from the torque converter to the tracks by means of the power train, which consists of the transmission, differential, final drives and sprockets.

b. Transmission. The transmission has two forward speeds and one reverse speed. Built into the transmission is the transmission brake, which is operated by the transmission brake pedal mounted on the floor to the left front of the driver (fig. 6). The function of the brake is to stall the torque converter (the engine must be at idling speed) when engaging or disengaging transmission gears.

c. Differential. The differential is called a "controlled differential" because it serves not only to transmit engine power to the final drive units but it also has a brake drum on each side of the differential housing for the purpose of steering and stopping the vehicle. The differential is so designed that when the speed of one brake drum is reduced, the speed of the other is increased.

63. ADJUSTMENT OF STEERING AND PARKING BRAKES.

a. The steering brake assemblies are located on either side of the differential between the end of the differential and the final drives. The adjustment of the steering brake is extremely important, and only specially qualified mechanics should be permitted to perform it.

64. LUBRICATION OF TRANSMISSION AND FINAL DRIVE.

a. Description.

(1) The oiling system for the transmission and final drive is a combination of the splash and pressure systems. The transmission, differential, and steering brakes are lubricated under pressure, while the final drive gear train is splash-lubricated.

(2) Located directly back of and beneath the compensating differential in the final drive housing is the oil sump. In this position the oil level remains constant on up or down gradients. Oil is screened and pumped to the rotor pump, which is located on the transmission and driven

POWER TRAIN

TM 9-721

by the transmission input shaft. Oil under pressure is forced through the final drive oil filter and cooler, located in the right rear sponson, and back to the distributor located on the front of the final drive housing. From the distributor, oil is pumped to the steering brakes, transmission and differential. A restriction valve insures oil to the transmission immediately after the engine is started.

b. Capacity and Grade of Oil.

(1) Combined transmission and final drive lubricating system holds a maximum of 40 gallons of oil. In general, OIL, lubricating, engine, SAE 30, should be used in winter, and OIL, lubricating, engine, SAE 50, should be used in the summer. For detailed information on grade of oils at varying degrees of temperature, refer to the lubrication guide furnished with each vehicle.

c. Filling and Draining Transmission and Final Drive.

(1) To fill the transmission and final drive lubricating system, first remove the filler plug at rear of final drive housing. Fill system with 40 gallons of the proper seasonal grade of oil. When the system is full, oil should level off at the filler plug.

(2) When filling a new transmission and final drive assembly, fill the final drive housing at the filler plug. Then, run the engine for approximately 20 minutes to fill oil cooler, oil filter, oil pipes and oil housing. Check oil level at filler plug and add oil to attain correct level. **NOTE:** It will be necessary to prime the oil sump at the initial start of the engine. In order to do so, disconnect the oil inlet to the oil pump and fill the suction hose with oil. Connect oil inlet to pump.

(3) Drain plugs are located in the bottom of the final drive housing, one at each end and one in the center. To drain oil from the transmission and final drive, remove all 3 drain plugs.

Section XIX

SUSPENSION AND TRACKS

	Paragraph
Description and operation	65
Bogie assembly	66
Removal of bogie assembly	67
Removal and installation of volute springs	68
Installation of bogie assembly	69
Tracks	70
Adjustment of track	71
Removing the track	72
Installing the track	73
Auxiliary idler	74
Track supporting rollers	75

65. DESCRIPTION AND OPERATION.

a. Eight four-wheeled, rubber-tired bogies or suspensions, bolted to the hull and to the track armor plate, support the vehicle on springs. The tracks are driven by twin sprockets mounted on the rear of the vehicle. Two twin, main, adjustable idlers at the front end of the hull are provided to maintain constant tension on the tracks. Two twin, auxiliary, nonadjustable idlers mounted between the main adjustable idlers and the front bogie assembly provide track support for the main idler and front bogie assembly when the vehicle is crossing rough terrain. On level ground the track does not touch the auxiliary idler. The weight of the upper portion of the track is carried by dual rubber track supporting rollers bolted between the track armor plate and the hull.

66. BOGIE ASSEMBLY.

a. Description and Operation. The bogie assemblies are the supporting and conveying units, and are sometimes called trucks or suspensions. Movement is transferred from wheels to arms and levers, and is absorbed by springs. Wear between wheel arms and spring lever is taken by plates which are removable, and can be replaced.

b. Lubrication. Lubrication of wheels and track supporting rollers is through lubrication fittings. Relief valves are provided to prevent injury to oil seals.

67. REMOVAL OF BOGIE ASSEMBLY.

a. Bogie assemblies are removed either for replacement, to repair tires, inspect or replace bearings, or to make other necessary repairs.

SUSPENSION AND TRACKS

TM 9-721
67

In removing the bogie assemblies from the Heavy Tanks M6 and M6A1, the track armor plate on the side of the vehicle interferes with the removal of the bogie assembly in normal fashion. To remove either the front or rear bogie assembly, it is necessary to disconnect the assembly, then slide it out from underneath the front or rear of the hull. To remove either of the center two bogie assemblies, it is necessary to remove first the front or rear bogie assembly, in order to provide a way to slide the center bogie assemblies out from under the hull. An alternate method of removing either of the two center bogie assemblies is to dig a pit under the bogie which is to be removed, and disconnect and drop the bogie into the pit. This will provide sufficient clearance for the bogie to pass underneath the track armor plate. *Do not attempt to remove the track armor plate except when absolutely necessary.* In addition to the excessive weight of the armor plate (1,865 lb) it is practically impossible to aline retaining screw holes when installing the armor plate.

b. **Removal of Bogie Assembly** (figs. 29, 30 and 36).

(1) Remove the 5 retaining screws which secure the outer bogie shaft lock plate to the track armor plate. Do not remove the 2 screws which hold the lower half of the bogie shaft lock plate in position.

(2) Remove the 2 clamp screws which secure the lower half of the

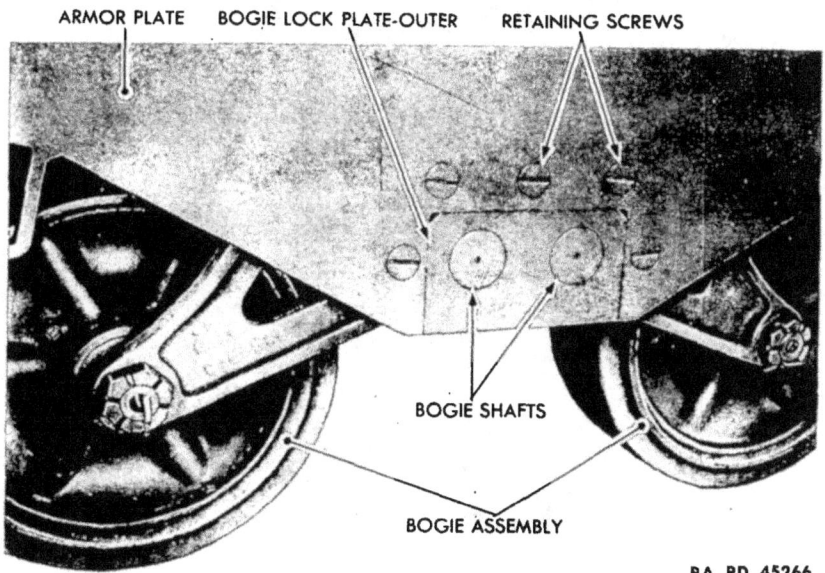

RA PD 45266

Figure 29 — Installed Bogie Assembly

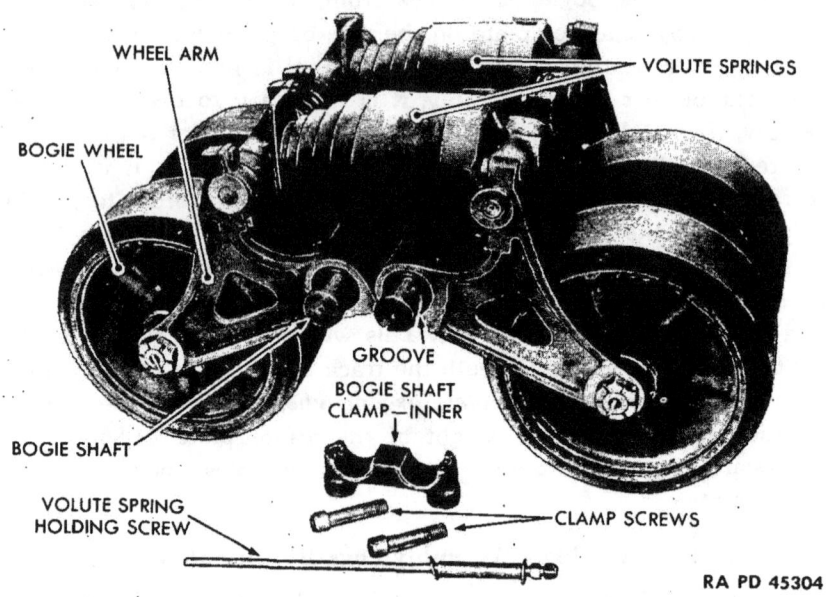

Figure 30 — View of Bogie Assembly

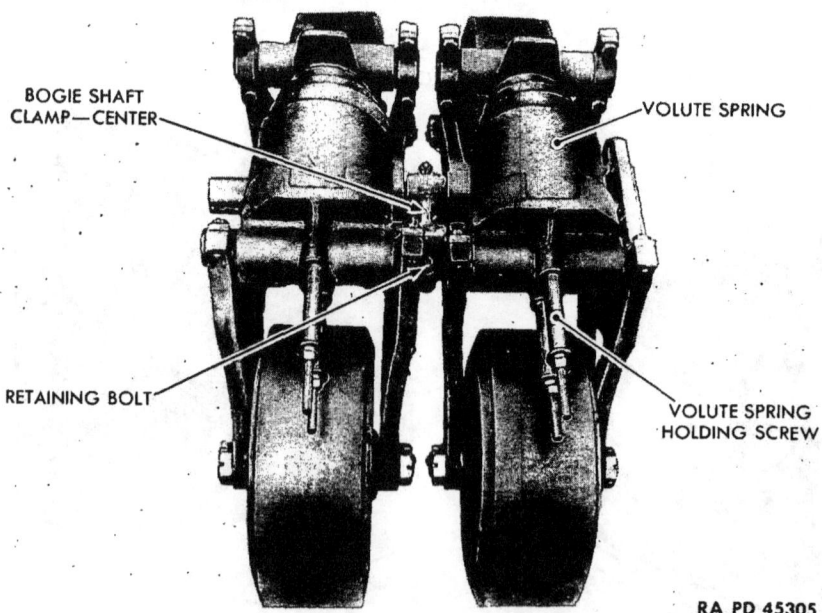

Figure 31 — Volute Spring Holding Screws in Position for Removal of Volute Springs

SUSPENSION AND TRACKS

inner bogie shaft lock plate to the upper half of the bogie shaft lock plate, which is bolted to the hull. Remove the bogie assembly from under the vehicle.

68. REMOVAL AND INSTALLATION OF VOLUTE SPRINGS (figs. 30 and 31).

a. Remove Volute Springs.

(1) Install 2 volute spring holding screws through each of the bogie assembly volute springs. Screws run from 1 wheel arm, through the volute spring, and screw into the opposite wheel arm. Tighten down all 4 volute spring holding screws.

(2) The inner bogie shaft lock plate should have been removed when the bogie assembly was removed from the vehicle. Remove the 2 clamp screws which secure the lower half of the outer bogie shaft lock plate to the upper half of the outer bogie shaft lock plate.

(3) Make sure volute spring holding screws are fixed securely in position, then remove the center bogie shaft clamp.

(4) Keeping the volute spring holding screws tightly threaded in the wheel arms, alternately loosen outer screws on the 4 volute spring holding screws. This will slowly separate the two halves of the bogie assembly, and will slowly relieve the tension of the volute springs. **CAUTION:** Take extreme care in performing this operation. Volute springs are under high tension and if bogie shaft clamps are removed without volute springs holding screws in position, the volute springs will fly out and may injure maintenance personnel performing operation.

b. Installation of Volute Springs (figs. 30 and 31).

(1) Install 4 volute spring holding screws in the bogie wheel arms. Slide volute springs over the screws. Install nuts on the volute holding screws. Tighten down nuts, bringing the two halves of the bogie assembly together, until the bogie shaft center clamp and outer lock plate may be installed.

(2) Install bogie shaft center clamp, then install the upper and lower halves of the outer bogie shaft lock plate. Make sure the 2 retaining screws which secure the lower half of the lock plate pass through the grooves in the bogie shafts.

69. INSTALLATION OF BOGIE ASSEMBLY (figs. 29, 30 and 36).

a. Place the bogie assembly in position underneath the vehicle between the track armor plate and hull.

b. Install the retaining screws which secure the outer bogie shaft lock plate to the track armor plate.

HEAVY TANKS M6 AND M6A1

c. Place the lower half of the inner bogie shaft lock plate in position and install the 2 clamp screws which secure it to the upper half of the shaft lock plate. Make sure the 2 clamp screws pass through the slots in the bogie shafts.

70. TRACKS (figs. 32 and 33).

a. **Description.** Each track on the vehicle is composed of a number of half rubber and half steel blocks. Tracks are double, the track block consisting of 2 blocks held together by 2 parallel connecting pins. Pins project from either end of the blocks, and are bare between the blocks, to form anchorage points for the end connectors, which link the blocks together on both sides to form a continuous track. The 2 end connectors are held to the pins by wedges which fit into knurled slots on the pins. These slots face outward, and are vertical to the flat side of the blocks. The wedges are tapered on each end so that when they are pulled up between the 2 pins by the bolt, which is an integral part of the wedge and which projects up through the connector, they cause an angle between adjacent blocks. This angle tends to make the block curve up sharply around the idler at the front of the vehicle and around the sprocket at the rear of the vehicle. Steel perpendicular end plates cast integral with the end connectors serve as guides to keep the blocks in line with the bogie wheels, idlers, track supporting rollers, and drive sprockets. The sprocket drives the track through the sprocket teeth, which engage the track between adjacent end connectors. A center connector is also used. This differs from the conventional type end connector in that it consists of two halves, which clamp around adjacent center pins, and are held together by a bolt and nut.

b. **Maintenance of Tracks.** Since the condition and effectiveness of the track can definitely limit or increase performance ability of a vehicle, it is essential that the track be regularly inspected, adjusted and maintained in the best possible conditions.

71. ADJUSTMENT OF TRACK.

a. Check the track daily for too much sag. If a pronounced sag is evident, correct the track tension to eliminate the possibility of the track being damaged or thrown off because of looseness. Provision to adjust the track is made at the main idler in the front of the vehicle. Since the main idler is dual, to accommodate the double track, it must be adjusted at both the outer and inner sides (figs. 35 and 36). In turning the adjusting idler jackscrews, alternately turn the inner and outer screws to prevent cocking the idler.

b. **Adjusting Track.**

(1) Remove the lock wire which secures the idler block nuts and the cover plate nuts (fig. 34).

SUSPENSION AND TRACKS

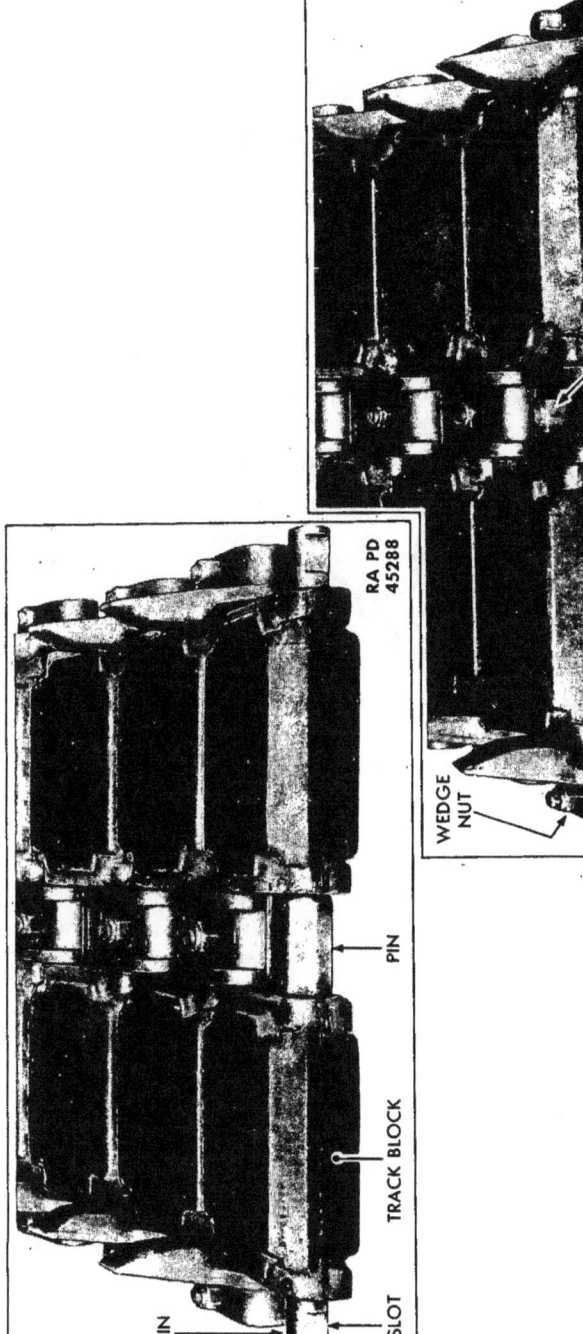

Figure 33—Track Block Assembly (Connectors Installed)

Figure 32—Track Block Assembly

TM 9-721
71 HEAVY TANKS M6 AND M6A1

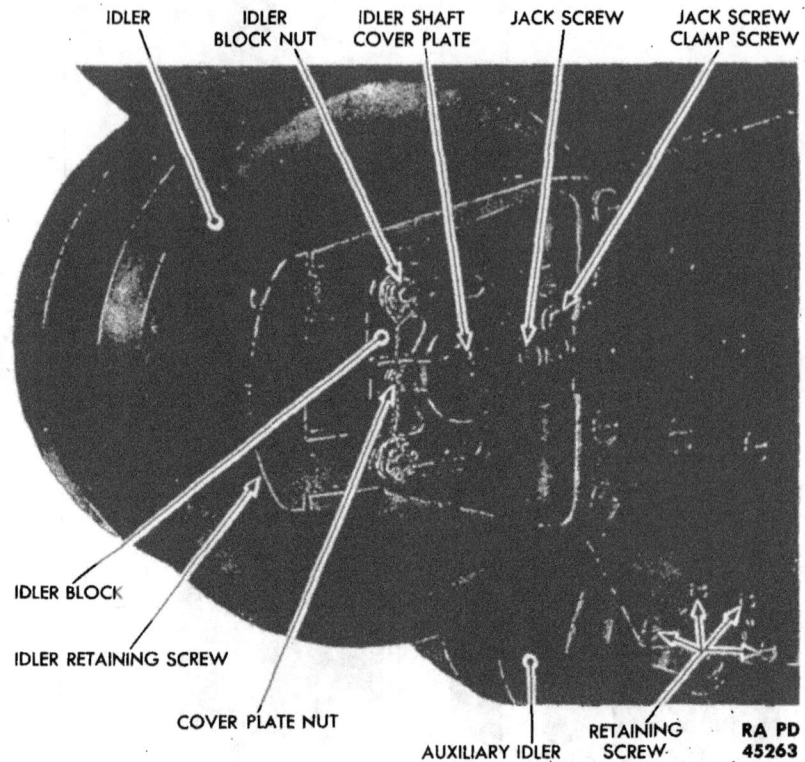

Figure 34—Detail of Idler Assembly

(2) Loosen the idler block nuts, then loosen the jackscrew clamp screws (fig. 34). Remove the cover plate nuts and lift off the idler shaft cover plates (fig. 34).

(3) Loosen the idler shaft screws (each side of the idler) (fig. 35).

(4) Alternating between the inner and outer jackscrews, turn the jackscrews in or out to move the idler in its slots in the idler block and adjust track tension (fig. 35).

(5) When the tension in the track has been adjusted, measure distance from the end of the idler block to the jackscrew clamp. This should be the same on both the inner and outer idler blocks, thus providing a check against the idler having been cocked when the inner and outer jackscrews were turned.

(6) Tighten the idler shaft screw, jackscrew clamp screw and idler blocknuts (fig. 34).

SUSPENSION AND TRACKS

TM 9-721
71-72

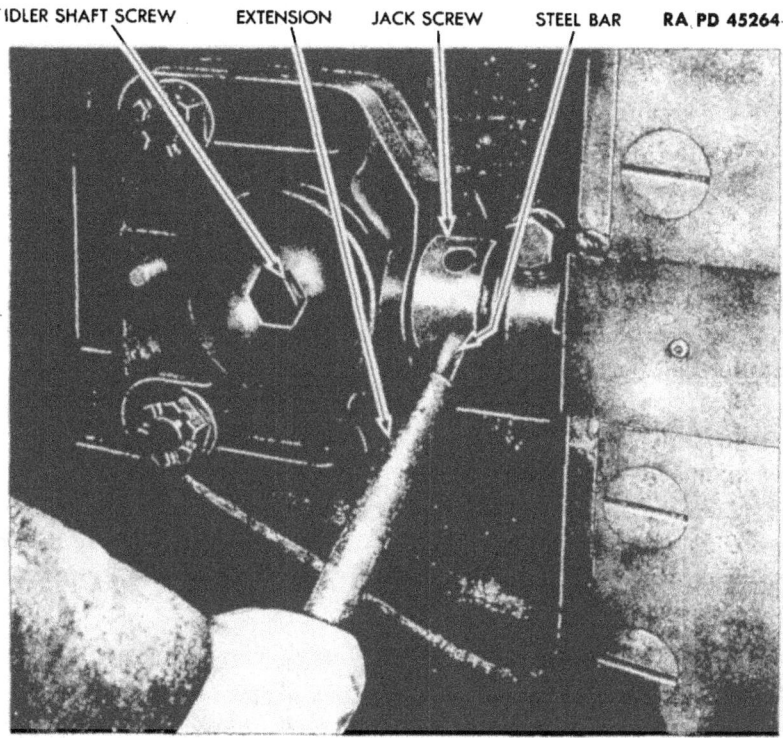

Figure 35 — Adjusting Track Tension

(7) Install the idler shaft cover plates and cover plate nuts. Lock wire idler block nuts and cover plate nuts.

72. REMOVING THE TRACK.

a. **Release Track Tension.** Release the tension on the track by turning in the jackscrews as far as possible. This will slide the idler back in its slots at the idler block (par. 71).

b. **Remove End Connectors.**

(1) Loosen and remove wedge nuts on corresponding inner and outer end connectors of the track that are midway between the main idler and front bogie wheel. Tap wedges out of end connectors, being careful not to injure the threads.

(2) Working from opposite sides of tracks from end connectors, and with point of bar against flange of end connectors, drive connectors off the track pins.

(3) Remove the bolt and nut which clamp the 2 wedges of the center connector together. Perform this operation to one side of the track, being careful that the track does not fly up and injure maintenance personnel.

c. **Remove Track.**

(1) Move the upper portion of the track to the rear of the supporting rollers and drive sprockets.

(2) Pull the vehicle off the tracks.

73. INSTALLING THE TRACK.

a. **Place Track in Position.**

(1) Lay out the track in front of the vehicle in a straight line with the main idler and bogie wheels. Hook a prime mover to the vehicle with a tow cable.

(2) Pull the vehicle forward on track until forward end of track is between main idler and auxiliary idler.

(3) Connect the cable to the rear end of the track. Run the cable over the sprocket, across the top of the supporting rollers and above the main idler. Hook the cable to the prime mover, then pull the track up and into position for connection.

b. **Connect Track.**

(1) Work the ends of the track together as close as possible. Place the track connecting fixture in position, and jack the ends of the track together.

(2) Place the two halves of the center track connector in position on the track pins, and install clamp bolt and nut.

(3) Drive end connectors on the pins, and install wedges and wedge nuts. Two to three threads must extend beyond the ends of the nuts to insure that the safety feature of the nut has a full grip. After assembly of wedges, there must be at least $\frac{1}{16}$-inch clearance between top of wedge and the end connectors.

c. **Adjust Track Tension.** Adjust track tension by means of the main idler at the front of the vehicle (par. 71).

74. AUXILIARY IDLER.

a. **Description.** A nonadjustable auxiliary idler is mounted between the main idler and front bogie assembly. The function of the auxiliary idler is to provide additional support for the track when the vehicle is crossing rough terrain. When the vehicle is operating on relatively smooth ground, the auxiliary idler does not touch the track.

b. **Removal of Auxiliary Idler** (figs. 34 and 36). Removal and

SUSPENSION AND TRACKS

TM 9-721
74-75

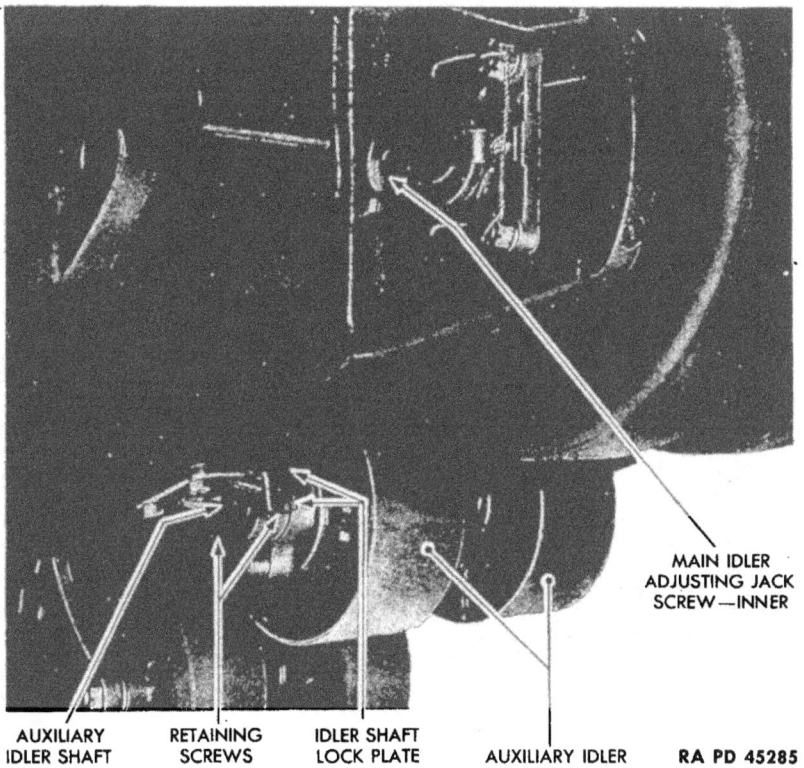

Figure 36 — Installed Auxiliary Idler

installation of the auxiliary idler is similar to that of removing and installing the bogie assemblies. Two clamp screws secure the lower half of the auxiliary idler shaft lock plate (inner and outer) to the upper half of the auxiliary lock plate (inner and outer). When these clamp screws are removed, the halves of the lock plate separate, releasing the auxiliary idler shaft.

75. TRACK SUPPORTING ROLLERS.

a. Description. Four, dual, track supporting rollers are mounted on each side of the vehicle to provide support for the upper half of the track. Rollers are bolted to track armor plate and to the hull.

b. Removal of Track Supporting Roller (fig. 37). Remove the retaining screws which secure the track supporting roller to the hull and to the track armor plate. Lift the track supporting roller up and out of the vehicle.

Figure 37 — Installed Track Supporting Roller

c. **Lubrication** (fig. 37). A lubrication fitting adaptable to a grease gun is installed in the end of the track supporting roller shaft. This projects through a hole drilled in the track armor plate, thus providing access to the lubrication fitting while the track is installed.

Section XX

ELECTRICAL SYSTEM

	Paragraph
Batteries	76
Auxiliary generating unit	77
Voltage regulator	78
Fuse box	79
Instrument panel	80
Maintenance of instruments	81
Lights	82
Trouble shooting	83

76. BATTERIES.

a. **General.** Due to the large number of electrically operated accessories, a 24-volt electrical system is installed in the Heavy Tanks M6 and M6A1.

b. **Description.** Two 12-volt storage batteries are connected in series to maintain the voltage of the system at 24 volts. The batteries are installed in two battery boxes located at the rear of the driving compartment (figs. 39 and 40). Battery box covers may be easily removed by removing the 2 wing nuts which secure each cover to the battery box. To remove the batteries, disconnect all battery cables, remove the nuts from battery, hold down bolts and lift out of the battery (fig. 40).

c. **Maintenance.**

(1) CARE. Check battery terminals and terminal posts frequently, clean and coat with PETROLATUM. Check the battery fluid level once a week and after every long run. Maintain the level to ¼ inch above the plate assemblies by adding distilled water. Take a specific gravity reading every 25 hours and exchange a battery having a specific gravity of 1.225 or less at 80 F, for one fully charged.

(2) CAPACITY AND TEMPERATURE DATA. At temperatures below freezing the load on the battery becomes greater, and the relative capacity of the battery is reduced. For this reason, when low temperatures prevail, it will be necessary to maintain the specific gravity of the battery electrolyte at 1.250 or higher, and to replace the battery when its gravity

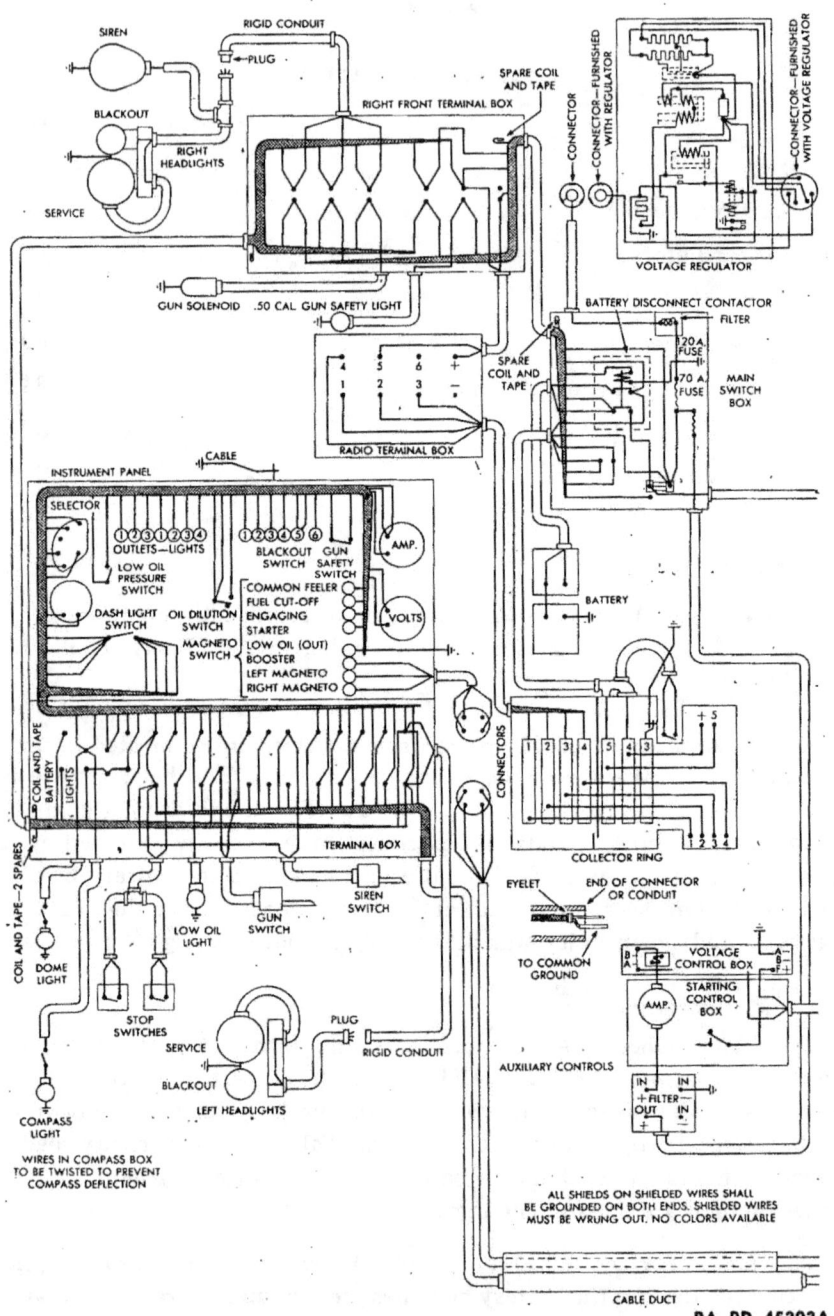

Figure 38 — Wiring Diagram — Hull

ELECTRICAL SYSTEM

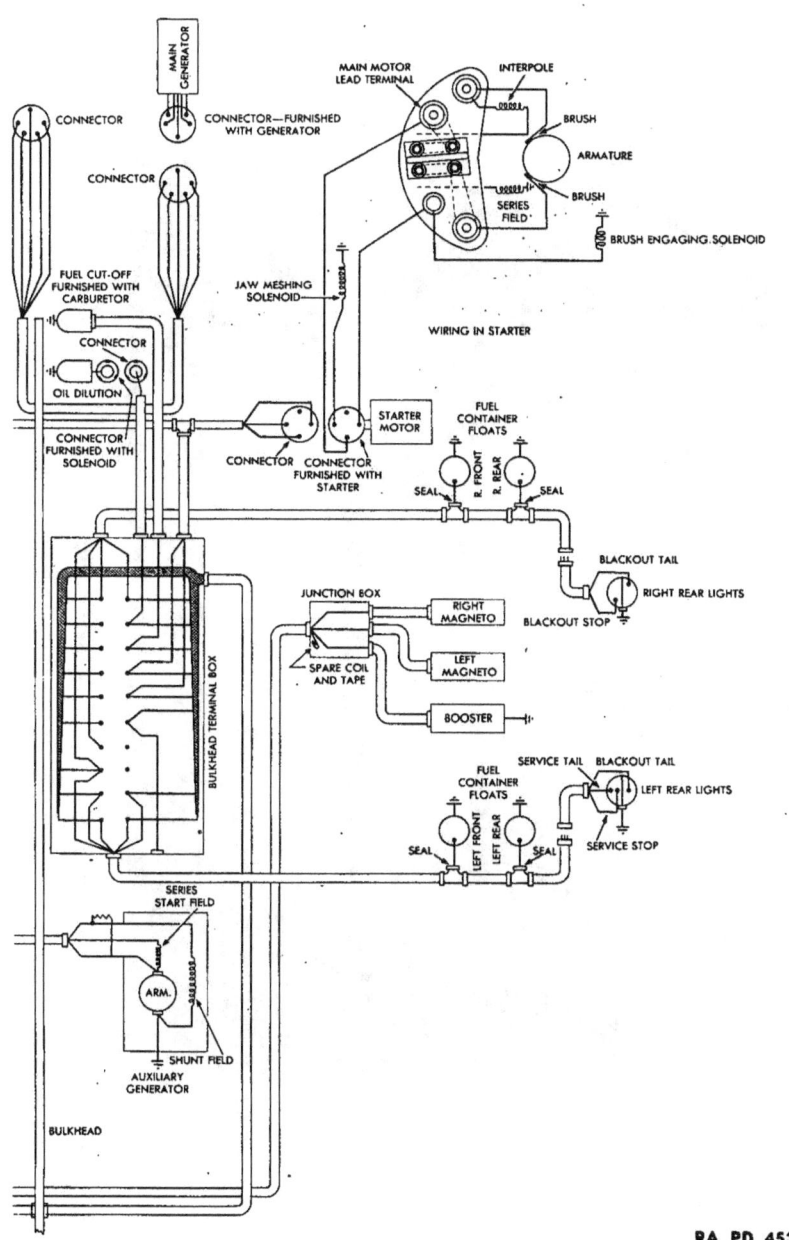

Figure 38 — Wiring Diagram — Hull

Figure 39 — Rear View of Driving Compartment

ELECTRICAL SYSTEM

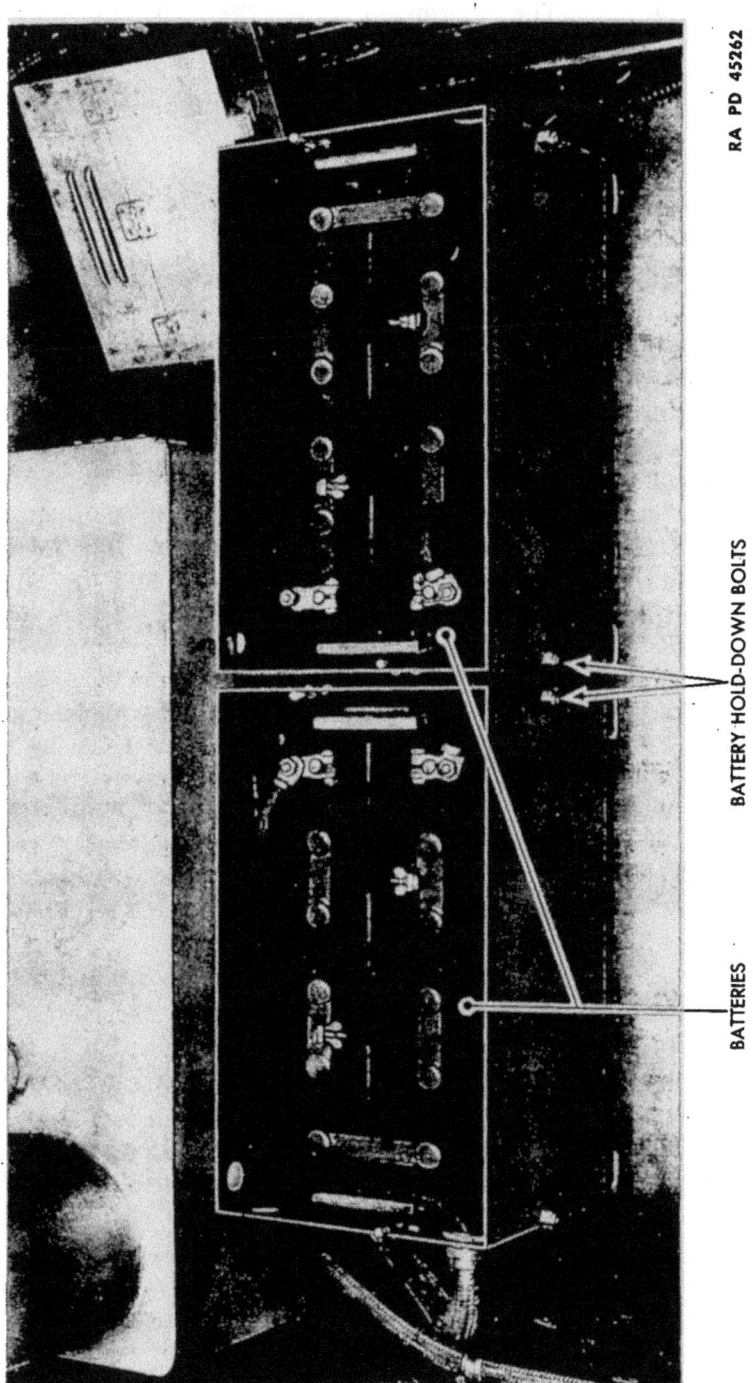

Figure 40—Installed Batteries

reading is below 1.225. The following data show the capacity of the batteries, and the relative freezing point of the electrolyte.

CAPACITY	ACTUAL SPECIFIC GRAVITY	FREEZING TEMPERATURE
Battery charged	1.285	−96 F
Battery ⅓ discharged	1.255	−60 F
Battery ½ discharged	1.220	−31 F
Battery ¾ discharged	1.185	− 8 F
Battery normally discharged	(1.150)	+ 5 F
	(1.100)	+18 F

(3) To determine the actual specific gravity of the electrolyte, it is necessary to check the temperature of the solution with a thermometer. If the temperature is normal (80 F) the specific gravity reading will be correct. However, if the temperature is above or below 80 F, it will be necessary to make an allowance to determine the actual specific gravity. This is due to the fact that the liquid expands when warm, and the same volume weighs less than when it is at normal temperature. The reverse is also true, and when the temperature is below normal or 80 F, the liquid has contracted and the same volume weighs more than it does when normal. To correct the specific gravity reading to make it correspond to the temperature of the electrolyte, add or subtract 0.004 from the hydrometer reading for each 10 degrees variation in temperature from the normal of 80 F. For example, when the specific gravity, as shown by the hydrometer reading, is 1.290 and the temperature of the electrolyte is 60 F, it will be necessary to subtract 8 points or 0.008 from 1.290 which gives 1.282 as the actual specific gravity. If the hydrometer reading shows 1.270, at a temperature of 110 F, it will be necessary to add 12 points or 0.012 to the reading which gives 1.282 as the actual specific gravity.

77. AUXILIARY GENERATING UNIT (figs. 41 and 42).

a. General.

(1) The auxiliary generating unit is a self-contained unit used for charging the tank batteries. The unit is located in the left rear sponson, and may be reached either from within the engine driving compartment or by removing the compartment plate recessed in the left track armor plate (fig. 41).

(2) The auxiliary generating unit should be in operation whenever the turret is being electrically operated, or when the guns are being fired (3-inch gun, 37-mm gun and bow cal. .30 machine gun are fired electrically).

b. Description.

(1) The unit consists of a 2-cycle, 2-volt, single-cylinder, air-cooled,

ELECTRICAL SYSTEM

TM 9-721
77

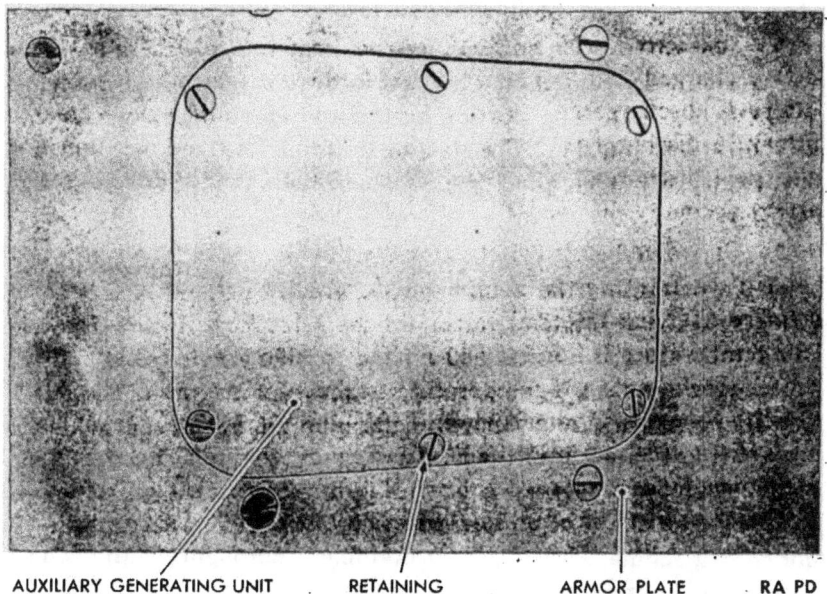

AUXILIARY GENERATING UNIT COMPARTMENT PLATE   RETAINING SCREWS   ARMOR PLATE (LEFT SIDE OF VEHICLE)   RA PD 45275

Figure 41 — Auxiliary Generating Unit Compartment Plate

AUXILIARY GENERATING UNIT   RA PD 45274

Figure 42 — Installed Auxiliary Generating Unit

inverted type gasoline engine operating at 3,500 to 3,600 revolutions per minute, and a 30-volt, 1,500-watt generator.

(2) The control box and voltage regulator unit for the auxiliary generating unit are mounted on a bracket in the left rear of the driving compartment (fig. 24). The starting button and an ammeter are located on the control box (fig. 24). The starting button is used only for starting the unit electrically. Charging rate of the generator is indicated by the ammeter.

(3) Choke and stop switches for the auxiliary generating unit project through the front engine compartment bulkhead, above and to the rear of the control box (fig. 43).

(4) Fuel for the auxiliary generating unit is carried in a fabric and synthetic rubber tank located in the left sponson in front of the left front main fuel tank (fig. 26). Access to the tank for filling is provided by a hinged armored fuel filler cover on the top of the hull (fig. 4). The fuel tank holds approximately 6 gallons of fuel, preferably a low octane gasoline. Fuel consists of a mixture of oil and gasoline, $\frac{3}{8}$ of a pint of OIL, lubricating, engine, SAE 40, 50 or 60 mixed thoroughly with each gallon of gasoline. Lubrication is provided by the oil mixed with the gasoline.

c. **Operation.**

(1) COLD WEATHER STARTING, BELOW 32 F.

(a) Close the carburetor choke (fig. 43).

(b) Depress starting button on control box (fig. 43). Release the button as soon as the engine starts and immediately open the choke partially easing to full open position as the engine warms up.

(2) WARM WEATHER STARTING, ABOVE 32 F.

(a) Depress the starting button on the control box (fig. 43). Release the button as soon as the engine starts.

(b) Do not use the choke unless the engine does not start within 5 seconds. If the engine does not start, use the choke as in previous instructions. NOTE: Do not use the choke as a throttle. The automatic governor operates the engine at the proper speed for all loads. No reading should show on the ammeter on the instrument panel when starting the auxiliary unit.

(3) STOPPING THE ENGINE.

(a) To stop the engine, press the stop button and hold it firmly closed till the engine stops (fig. 43). Close fuel line shut-off valve.

78. VOLTAGE REGULATOR.

a. **Description.**

(1) Two voltage controls are provided to prevent overcharging of batteries. The engine generator voltage regulator is located on the front

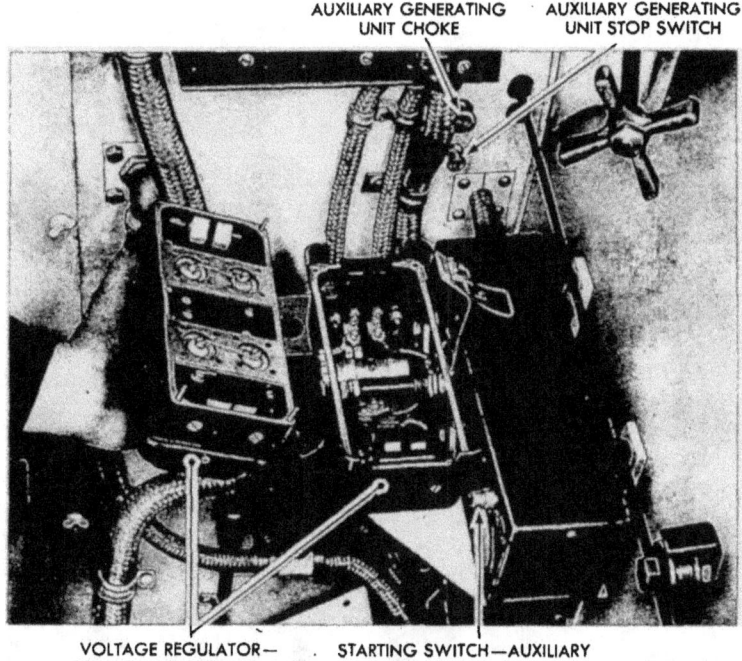

Figure 43 — Detail of Auxiliary Generating Unit Voltage Regulator

engine compartment bulkhead inside the driving compartment (fig. 39). The auxiliary generating unit voltage regulator is mounted on a bracket beneath and in front of the engine generator voltage control (fig. 39).

(2) The voltage regulating units maintain the output of the generators at a constant, predetermined voltage. The current output of the generators is automatically varied in accordance with the state of charge of the batteries and the amount of current being used throughout the vehicle. Thus the proper charge is delivered to the batteries at all times without danger of overcharging.

(3) The current limitator units limit the maximum current output of the batteries to a value slightly in excess of the rated capacities of the auxiliary generating unit and the engine generator.

(4) The reverse current relay or cut-out prevents the battery from discharging through either of the generators when the generators are at rest, or when they are developing less than normal voltage.

TM 9-721
78-79 HEAVY TANKS M6 AND M6A1

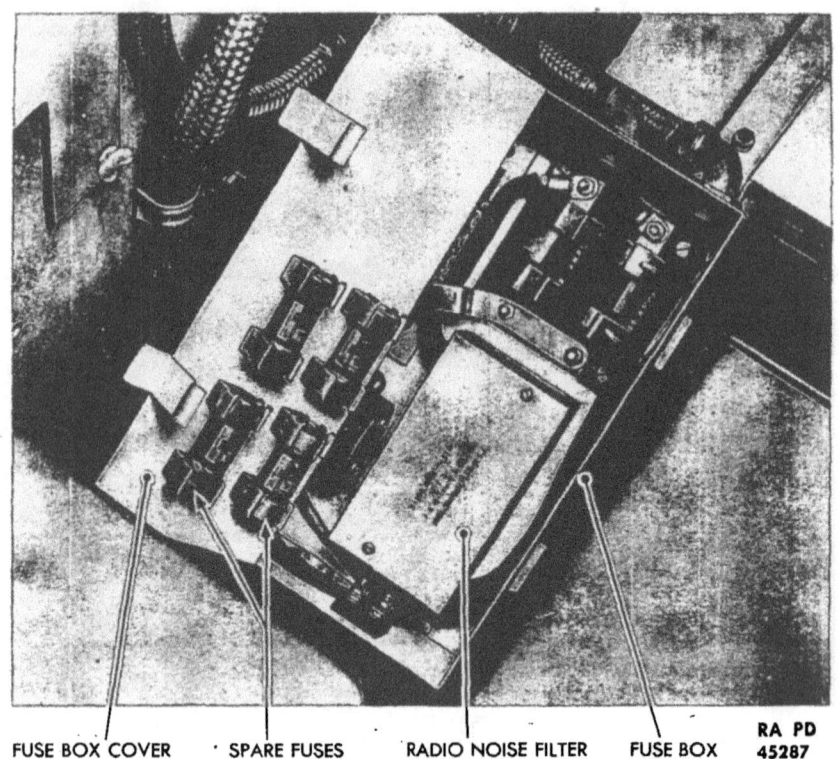

FUSE BOX COVER · SPARE FUSES · RADIO NOISE FILTER · FUSE BOX

RA PD 45287

Figure 44—Generator and Auxiliary Generator Voltage Regulators Fuse Box

b. **Inspection and Adjustments.** When properly installed and operated, the generator control units should not require adjustments. If inspection reveals loose or faulty contacts, improper operation of any type or if the voltage as indicated by the voltmeter is above or below normal, replace the unit (fig. 43). CAUTION: Before attempting to inspect or replace voltage regulators, make sure the battery switch is open.

79. **FUSE BOX** (figs. 39 and 44).

a. A fuse box, designed to prevent overloading of the voltage regulator circuits, is located on a slant on the floor of the left rear of the driving compartment. In the event of an overload or short circuit, fuses burn through, breaking the circuits. To install new fuses, open the fuse box door, remove the burned-out fuse and install new fuses. Spare fuses are carried in clips on the fuse box cover (fig. 44).

ELECTRICAL SYSTEM

80. INSTRUMENT PANEL (fig. 7).

a. General. The instrument panel is located at eye level to the left of the driver on the sponson wall, and contains the following electrical and non-electrical instruments, meters and switches:

(1) SPEEDOMETER. The speedometer is driven by a flexible shaft connecting from the gear and output shaft of the transmission. Two odometers, one showing trip mileage and the other showing total mileage, are incorporated in the head of the speedometer. The trip mileage speedometer reset is located on the instrument panel just above the speedometer.

(2) TACHOMETER. The speed of revolution of the engine crankshaft is indicated by the tachometer. It is driven by a flexible shaft connecting to the tachometer drive and the accessory-end of the engine. An engine hour meter is located in the face of the tachometer.

(3) HYCON PRESSURE GAGE. Pressure in the Hycon pressure tank is indicated by this gage.

(4) IGNITION SWITCH ASSEMBLY.

(a) The ignition switch assembly, mounted on the instrument panel, comprises five separate switches. The magneto switch at the top of the assembly has four positions as indicated on the switch. To extreme left—both magnetos off; to the left of center—right magneto on; to the right of center—left magneto on; to the extreme right—both magnetos on.

(b) An energized starter switch is mounted on the center of the assembly. The switch is used to energize the starting motor before the starting switch is applied. It is a pull-out type switch which snaps back automatically when released.

(c) To the left and right of the energized starter switch are mounted, respectively, the booster and starter switches. These are toggle type switches which swing outward in the "OFF" position. Direction of movements for starting the engine are indicated on the ignition switch assembly by arrows.

(d) Beneath the energized starting switch is located the fuel cut-off switch. This is also a toggle type switch which swings to the left in the "OFF" position.

(5) GUN SAFETY SWITCH. The gun safety switch is a pull-out type switch which acts as a safety switch to control firing of the bow cal. .30 machine gun. In order to fire the machine gun, this switch must be on.

(6) OIL DILUTION SWITCH. The oil dilution switch is a toggle switch

HEAVY TANKS M6 AND M6A1

which is used to operate the oil dilution system. Operating directions are mounted on the instrument panel beneath the switch.

(7) LIGHT SWITCH. The light switch is of the push-pull type. To operate the switch, the spring button on the side of the switch must be depressed. In addition to "OFF," the switch has three positions. The first operates blackout light; the second operates only the service headlights, and the third operates the service stop lights.

(8) CLOCK. Mounted in the center of the instrument panel to the right of the light switch is an 8-day clock. A second hand is also provided. Stem winder is at the base of the clock.

(9) CYLINDER TEMPERATURE GAGE. The cylinder temperature gage, graduated from 0 F to 600 F, is mounted on the center right of the instrument panel. Temperatures existing in the No. 1 cylinder during operation are indicated on the gage.

(10) ENGINE OIL TEMPERATURE GAGE. This gage indicates the engine oil temperature.

(11) ENGINE OIL PRESSURE GAGE. This gage records the pressure in the engine oil manifold.

(12) CONVERTER FLUID TEMPERATURE GAGE. This gage indicates the temperature of the operating fluid in the converter fluid system.

(13) CONVERTER OIL PRESSURE GAGE. This gage records the pressure of the fluid in the converter fluid system.

(14) FUEL GAGE. The fuel gage is mounted on the lower right side of the instrument panel. Directly above the fuel gage is a fuel tank selector. By switching the fuel tank selector to any of the fuel tanks indicated on the selector, quantity of gasoline in the tank may be recorded on the fuel gage.

(15) VOLTMETER. A voltmeter indicates the voltage in the circuit. A warning line on the voltmeter at the number 22 indicates when to switch on the auxiliary generating unit.

(16) AMMETER. The ammeter indicates the amount of current in amperes charging to or discharging from the battery. The amount of current will vary depending upon engine speed and electrical units in use.

(17) FINAL DRIVE OIL PRESSURE GAGE. This indicates the oil pressure of the oil circulating throughout the final drives.

(18) FINAL DRIVE OIL TEMPERATURE GAGE. This records the temperature of the oil circulating throughout the final drives.

(19) TRANSMISSION OIL PRESSURE GAGE. This records the pressure of the oil circulating throughout the transmission.

(20) DASH LIGHT SWITCH. The dash light switch is of the push-pull type, and is located in the right corner of the instrument panel.

ELECTRICAL SYSTEM

TM 9-721
80-82

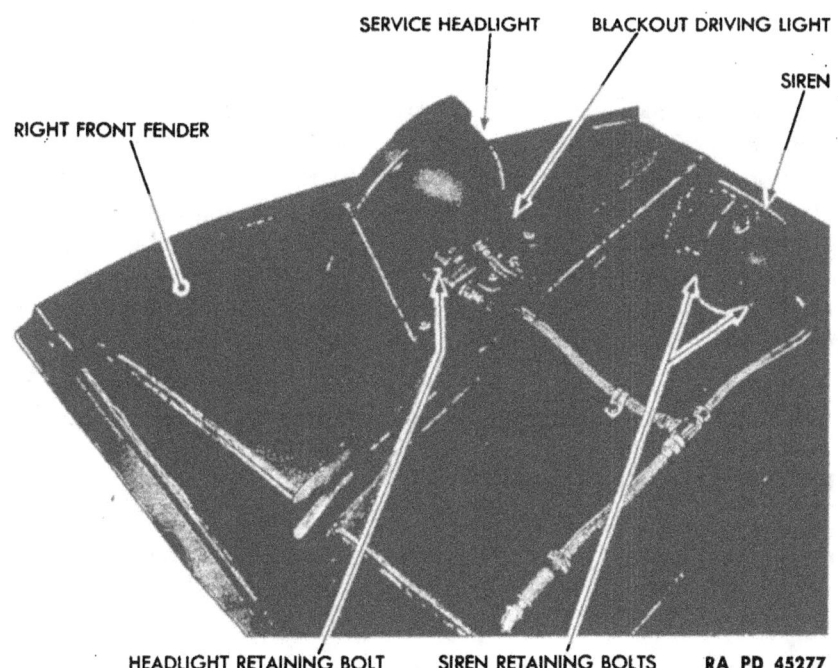

Figure 45—Detail of Headlight and Siren Installation

(21) SOCKETS. Three electrical sockets are provided in the instrument panel for use in conjunction with defroster, windshield wipers and trouble light.

(22) MAIN ELECTRICAL SWITCH. Four main electrical switches are grouped together at the extreme lower right-hand side of the instrument panel. These control vehicle lighting, coils, bow cal. .30 machine gun and the battery.

81. MAINTENANCE OF INSTRUMENTS.

a. All instruments and switches that become inoperative should be exchanged for serviceable instruments and switches.

82. LIGHTS (fig. 45).

a. **Headlights.** Two headlights are provided, one mounted on each of the front fenders. Headlights are focused by means of the focusing screw at the base of the light. Lights are removed by removing electrical connections, and removing the retaining bolt which secures the bracket on the base of the headlight to the bracket attached to the fender.

b. Blackout Lights. A blackout light is located beside each headlight. They are 3-candlepower lights.

c. Tail Lamps (fig. 1). Tail lamps are combination lamps. The rear left is the combination stop service and blackout lamp. The lower lens is a service and service stop light, and the upper lens is the blackout light. In the right rear light, a lower lens is the blackout light and the upper lens is the blackout stop light. Both stop lights are controlled by stop light switches incorporated in the manual steering levers and the Hycon controls. No stop signalling will be seen until both levers and controls are operated simultaneously, indicating a slowing up or full stop.

d. Siren (fig. 45). The siren is located on the right front fender and is actuated by a button located at the heel of the driver's foot rest.

83. TROUBLE SHOOTING.

a. General. Trouble shooting procedure in the electrical system is largely concerned with checking the wiring to make sure that it is serviceable. All grounded wires or wires that have open circuits must be replaced with wires of the same size and color.

b. Test Light. To test wiring requires a test light such as a 24-volt instrument panel light, a socket, two pieces of insulated wire (each about 18 in. in length), a clamp, a metal prod approximately an inch long, and tape. Install the light in the socket and connect one of the wires to the lead on the socket. Attach the metal clamp to the other end of the wire. Place tape over connection. Solder the end of the second wire to the side of the socket. To the other end of this wire connect the metal prod and place tape over the connection. **NOTE:** If a prod and a clamp are not available, scrape approximately an inch of insulation from each of the wires on the ends to which the clamp and prod should be attached. If no soldering equipment is available, scrape off several inches of insulation from the end of the wire which should be soldered to the side of the socket; wrap the end around the outside of the socket and place tape over the connection.

c. Jumper. Trouble shooting on the electrical system requires a jumper, which can be made by hooking up metal clamps on either end of a piece of insulated wire about 18 inches long. If clamps are not available, scrape off an inch of insulation from each end of the wire.

d. Testing of Wire. To test a wire for an open circuit or whether it is grounded on the vehicle, use the following procedure:

(1) Disconnect both ends of wire.

ELECTRICAL SYSTEM

(2) Hook up one end of test light to a positive lead and connect other end to one free end of the wire to be tested. If light burns, the wire is grounded on vehicle and should be replaced. If light does not burn, the wire is not grounded. To determine if a wire has an open circuit, proceed to next step.

(3) Ground the free end of wire being tested on the vehicle. If light burns, the wire is all right. If light does not burn, the wire has an open circuit and should be replaced.

e. Replacing Defective Wire.
(1) With current off, disconnect defective wire at both ends.
(2) Attach end of old wire to end of new wire, soldering them securely.
(3) Pull new wire in place by slowly drawing old wire out.
(4) Disconnect the two wires.
(5) Hook up new wire at both ends. **NOTE:** In replacing wire, be sure to install new wire of the same size and color as old wire.

f. Voltage Regulator. If voltmeter needle goes above 28.4 volts, the voltage regulator in the control box has failed. Report to proper authorities.

g. Starter Solenoid. If engine does not turn over, and voltmeter reads 28 or over, trouble in the starter solenoid or in the starter solenoid circuit is indicated. Check circuit for defective wires. Check ground connection on solenoid for loose connection. Check bridge between solenoid terminals, using a test light. If test reveals no trouble, the solenoid starter switch is defective and should be replaced.

h. Booster. If engine will not start, it may be due to failure of the booster. To check, use following procedure:
(1) One man should turn on the booster switch.
(2) Another man, at the engine compartment, should listen for the buzz of the points on the booster. If there is no buzz, proceed to step (3).
(3) Check wiring. If defective wire is found, it must be replaced. If no defective wire is found, the booster has failed. Report to proper authorities.

i. Spark Plugs. If engine is "missing," it may be due to defective spark plugs. To locate defective plug or plugs, apply a few drops of oil on the exhaust of each cylinder. Run engine. On those cylinders that are firing properly, the oil will disappear in a short time. On cylinders where the oil does not disappear, the cylinders are not firing properly. Remove wire from inoperative plug, hold ¼ inch away from good ground, and if spark indicates current is reaching plug, remove and replace plug.

j. Magneto. Following is a trouble shooting chart that should be used for locating and correcting magneto troubles.

(1) Engine Fails to Run on Magneto.

Probable Cause	Probable Remedy
Points not making proper contact.	Clean, check and adjust gap.
Point clearance too large.	Check and adjust gap.
Defective breaker assembly.	Replace magneto.
Defective coil assembly.	Replace magneto.
Shorted primary.	Disconnect switch wire. If magneto operates wire to switch, or switch is grounded, locate and clear trouble. If magneto does not operate, fault is in magneto. Replace magneto.

(2) Sudden Engine Failure.

Ground in switch or wire to switch.	Disconnect switch wire from magneto.
Defective breaker assembly.	Replace magneto.

(3) Engine Will Not Stop.

Broken switch wire.	Stop engine by shutting off fuel. Disconnect switch wire and ground out magneto. Replace switch wire.

(4) Loss of or No Power.

Ignition timing late.	Retime ignition.
Magneto weak.	Replace magneto.
Magneto internal timing incorrect.	Replace magneto.

(5) Rough Idling.

Ignition timing too far advanced.	Retime ignition.

(6) Misfiring at Low Speeds.

Breaker gap too large.	Check and adjust gap.
Magneto dirty.	Clean or replace.
Improperly adjusted.	Replace magneto.
Loose connections.	Make proper connections.
Weak magneto.	Replace magneto.
Other internal defects.	Replace magneto.

(7) Misfiring at High Speeds.

Breaker gap too small.	Check and adjust gap.
Defective breaker assembly.	Replace magneto.
Internal defects.	Replace magneto.

k. General Trouble Shooting. If, when the switch for any electrical unit is turned on, and the unit does not work, make the following check:

(1) Check battery switch to make sure it is closed.

ELECTRICAL SYSTEM

(2) Depress starter and watch ammeter and voltmeter to make sure current is coming from the battery. If ammeter does not show a discharge, the battery may need to be charged or replaced.

(3) Check for blown-out fuse.

(4) Check the electrical unit involved for failure. In case of lights, the light would be removed and tested or inspected for failure. Replace any defective units.

(5) Check wiring and replace defective wires.

(6) Check with test light at input terminal of unit to determine if current is flowing to unit. If circuit is operating, replace unit. If no current is reaching unit, check lead from current source to unit to locate ground or short.

Section XXI

PAINTING

	Paragraph
General	84
Preparing for painting	85
Painting metal surfaces	86
Paint as a camouflage	87
Removing paint	88
Painting lubricating devices	89

84. GENERAL.

a. Ordnance materiel is painted before issue to the using arms, and one maintenance coat per year will ordinarily be ample for protection. With but few exceptions, this materiel will be painted with **ENAMEL**, synthetic, olive-drab, lusterless. The enamel may be applied over old coats of long oil enamel and oil paint previously issued by the Ordnance Department if the old coat is in satisfactory condition for repainting.

b. Paints and enamels are usually issued ready for use and are applied by brush or spray. They may be brushed on satisfactorily when used unthinned in the original package consistency or when thinned no more than 5 percent by volume with thinner. The enamel will spray satisfactorily when thinned with 15 percent by volume of thinner. (OIL, linseed, must not be used as a thinner since it will impart a luster not desired in this enamel.) If sprayed, it dries hard enough for repainting within ½ hour and dries hard in 16 hours.

c. Certain exceptions to the regulations concerning painting exist. Fire-control instruments, sighting equipment, and other items which require a crystalline finish will not be painted with **ENAMEL**, olive-drab.

d. Complete information on painting is contained in TM 9-850.

85. PREPARING FOR PAINTING.

a. If the base coat on the materiel is in poor condition, it is more desirable to strip the old paint from the surface than to use sanding and touch-up methods. After stripping, it will then be necessary to apply a primer coat.

b. **PRIMER**, ground, synthetic, should be used on wood as a base coat for **ENAMEL**, synthetic. It may be applied either by brushing or spraying. It will brush satisfactorily as received or after the addition of not more than 5 percent by volume of thinner. It will be dry enough to touch in 30 minutes, and hard in 5 to 7 hours. For spraying, it may be thinned with not more than 15 percent by volume of thinner. Lacquers

PAINTING

must not be applied to the PRIMER, ground, synthetic, within less than 48 hours.

c. PRIMER, synthetic, rust-inhibiting, for bare metal is used on metal as a base coat. Its use and application are similar to that outlined in paragraph b above.

d. The success of a job of painting depends partly on the selection of a suitable paint, but also largely upon the care used in preparing the surface prior to painting. All parts to be painted should be free from rust, dirt, grease, kerosene, oil and alkali, and must be dry.

86. PAINTING METAL SURFACES.

a. If metal parts are in need of cleaning, they should be washed in a liquid solution consisting of ½ pound of SODA ASH in 8 quarts of warm water, or an equivalent solution, then rinsed in clear water and wiped thoroughly dry. Wood parts in need of cleaning should be treated in the same manner, but the alkaline solution must not be left on for more than a few minutes and the surfaces should be wiped dry as soon as they are washed clean. When artillery or automotive equipment is in fair condition and marred only in spots, the bad places should be touched with ENAMEL, synthetic, olive-drab, lusterless, and permitted to dry. The whole surface will then be sandpapered with PAPER, flint, No. 1, and a finish coat of ENAMEL, synthetic, olive-drab, lusterless, applied and allowed to dry thoroughly before the materiel is used. If the equipment is in bad condition, all parts should be thoroughly sanded with PAPER, flint, No. 2, or equivalent, given a coat of PRIMER, ground, synthetic, and permitted to dry for at least 16 hours. They will then be sandpapered with PAPER, flint, No. 00, wiped free from dust and dirt, and a final coat of ENAMEL, synthetic, olive-drab, lusterless, applied and allowed to dry thoroughly before the materiel is used.

87. PAINT AS A CAMOUFLAGE.

a. Camouflage is now a major consideration in painting ordnance vehicles, with rust prevention secondary. The camouflage plan at present employed, utilizes three factors: Color, gloss, and stenciling. Vehicles are painted with ENAMEL, synthetic, olive-drab, lusterless, which was chosen to blend in reasonably well with the average landscape.

88. REMOVING PAINT.

a. After repeated paintings, the paint may become so thick as to crack and scale off in places, presenting an unsightly appearance. If such is the case, remove the old paint by use of a lime and lye solution (see TM 9-850 for details) or paint and varnish remover. It is important that every trace of lye or other paint remover be completely rinsed off and that the equipment be perfectly dry before repainting is attempted. It is preferable that the use of lye solutions be limited to iron or steel parts. If used on wood, the lye solution must not be allowed to remain on the surface for more than a minute before being thoroughly rinsed off and the surface wiped dry with rags. Crevices or cracks in wood should be filled with putty and the wood sandpapered before refinishing. The surfaces thus prepared should be painted according to directions in paragraph 86.

89. PAINTING LUBRICATING DEVICES.

a. Oil cups, grease fittings, oilholes, and similar lubricating devices, as well as a circle about ¾ inch in diameter at each point of lubrication will be painted with **ENAMEL**, red, water-resisting, in order that they may be readily located.

Section XXII

SHIPMENT AND STORAGE

	Paragraph
Shipment	90
Preparation for storage	91
Storage of components and equipment	92

90. SHIPMENT.

a. When shipping the Heavy Tanks M6 and M6A1, by rail on flat cars, every precaution must be taken to have the vehicles properly fastened and blocked to the floor of the car.

b. Cars must be inspected to see if they are in a suitable condition to carry the load safely to its destination. The weight of the vehicle (64 tons) makes it most necessary that the cars have good sound floors. All loose nails or other projections not an integral part of the car, other than the prescribed blocking, must be removed. Loose nails, bolts, etc., necessary in car construction, should be made tight rather than removed.

c. The load must be so distributed that there will not be more weight on one side of the car than on the other. If a single vehicle is placed on a car, it must be so located that one truck of the carrying car does not carry more than one-half of the load weight. All doors and other openings should be closed and securely fastened as a protection against weather and pilfering of equipment. Material used for blocking must be of hardwood, fir, spruce, or long leaf yellow pine, straight grain and free from strength-impairing knots.

d. If the vehicle is to be used immediately upon reaching its destination, it may be desirable to keep the fuel tanks filled. If transportation is by rail express, in which case civilian passengers may be carried in coaches of the same train, the fuel tanks must be drained. The draining of the fuel tanks is not required if only military personnel is carried in accompanying coaches.

e. The handbrakes should be applied as soon as the vehicle is properly located on the car top. There must be at least 6 inches clearance in back, on both sides, of and above the handbrake.

f. Equipment moving from manufacturer to arsenal or proving ground, or from arsenal or proving ground to army post, or individual units moving from one army post to another *must* be placarded "DO NOT HUMP."

g. Further details on loading are to be found in "Special Supplement Containing Rules Governing The Loading Of Mechanized And Motorized

Army Equipment, Also, Major Caliber Guns For The United States Army And Navy, On Open Top Equipment," published by the Association of American Railroads, Operations and Maintenance Department, April 1, 1941. Field Manual No. 101-10 also gives information on shipping instructions.

h. Before fastening the vehicle to the car, it will be necessary to take certain measures to prevent corrosion during transit. If the vehicle is to be in transit for a period of not more than 30 days, it will be permissible to prepare it by operating the engine for a minimum period of one hour, on unleaded white gasoline. However, if it is at all practicable, spraying of the interior of the engine with corrosion-preventive compound, according to the methods outlined in AR 850-18 is desirable. This will not be possible without first removing the engine. If the vehicle is to be put in dead storage after it reaches its destination, the engine should be removed and shipped separately in order that corrosion-preventive treatment can be applied immediately before shipment and shortly after it reaches its destination and is placed in dead storage. Due to the corrosive nature of the high octane gasoline ordinarily used in the engine, it is most necessary that the above-mentioned corrosion-preventive measures be taken. Failure to do so will result in serious damage by corrosion. The following paragraph will outline the methods of applying corrosion-preventive compounds.

91. PREPARATION FOR STORAGE.

a. **General Instructions.** The storage of motor vehicles and equipment and inspection in connection therewith are covered in AR 850-18. It will not be practicable in many cases to apply the internal corrosion-preventive treatment to the vehicle prior to limited storage because of the difficulty in removing spark plugs and spraying the interiors of cylinders and other parts while the engine is installed. Insofar as it is possible to do so, methods outlined in AR 850-18 must be followed in order that engines and other portions of the materiel are properly protected from damage by corrosion; for dead storage engines must be removed from the vehicle, inspected, reconditioned, if necessary, and then given the proper corrosion-preventive treatment and stored separately.

b. **Storage Conditions.** Vehicles which are not in actual use will be stored in closed buildings or covered sheds if available. In lieu of this preferred storage space, they may be stored in the open and covered with tarpaulins. In each case, the floor must be solid and free from crushed rock, deep dust, and oil surfacing. It is desirable that tracks rest on planks. Every precaution must be taken to afford proper drainage of water from the floor and to locate the place of storage so that the materiel will be properly protected from flood or fire.

SHIPMENT AND STORAGE

c. **Technical Inspections.** The vehicles and equipment will be inspected at the time they are placed in storage and at frequent periods as designated in AR 850-18. A tag or tags tied to the unit or vehicle will be kept up to date by the inspector, indicating the condition and work to be done before the unit is again placed in service. Minor work of surface preservation and application of corrosion-preventives will be accomplished at the time of inspection. Work involving the use of shop facilities will be accomplished at the earliest practicable date. Batteries should be removed when a vehicle is placed in dead storage and the battery placed in active stock if practicable.

d. **Limited Storage.** Vehicles in limited storage are those that are out of service for less than 30 days. Vehicles stored under this heading will be ready for immediate service, and the fuel tanks and oil tanks will be kept filled. The batteries will be maintained in a fully charged condition and should remain in the vehicle. The battery switch and radio switch will be open during storage periods. The vehicle must be thoroughly cleaned and lubricated before being placed in limited storage, and proper precautions should be taken to protect the rubber elements from extreme light or heat. Brakes will not be left applied and the vehicle will not be left in gear.

e. **Placing Vehicles in Dead Storage.** Vehicles in dead storage are those that will not be required for service for an indefinite period. Vehicles should not be in limited storage status for over 30 days; however, it will be impossible to rigidly adhere to this ruling under certain combat conditions. When the vehicle is placed in dead storage, the engine will be removed, inspected, repaired at once if practicable, and treated with corrosion-preventive compound. In any event, it is most essential that the treatment with corrosion-preventive compounds be given immediately after the engine is placed in dead storage.

(1) ENGINE (VALVE COMPARTMENT). Remove the rocker box covers and spray the valve mechanism with corrosion-preventive compound. Special spraying outfits are available for applying this compound. The engine crankshaft will be rotated while the corrosion-preventive compound is applied in such a manner as to thoroughly cover the entire surface of cams and protruding ends of valve stems.

(2) CYLINDERS. The cylinder walls, piston heads and valves will be treated with corrosion preventive compound. The engine shall be set with the crankshaft extending vertically upward, with the piston of the cylinder being sprayed, placed on bottom center of the suction stroke. Each cylinder shall be sprayed through the spark plug hole, taking care not to damage the threads during the spraying operation. The quantity of compound to be sprayed into each cylinder will be metered, if possible;

if meters are not available, measurement will be accomplished by accurately determining the time required to spray the specific quantities and timing subsequent spraying of the individual cylinder to obtain the proper quantity in each. Personnel first performing the spraying operation shall determine by experiment the proper technique for completely coating cylinder wall, piston head and valves with corrosion-preventive compound. Two ounces ($\frac{1}{8}$ pint) of compound will be sprayed into each cylinder, after which the engine crankshaft will be revolved at least two complete revolutions. The cylinder space above each piston will then be resprayed with $\frac{1}{16}$ pint (1 ounce) of compound, without revolving the crankshaft further, since this space is particularly susceptible to corrosion. This procedure permits treatment of the maximum surface of the cylinder wall and the piston head. The intake valve will be open sufficiently to permit a small quantity of the vaporized corrosion-preventive compound to reach the valve face. After thus treating the interior of all cylinders, a small quantity of the corrosion-preventive compound will be sprayed into each exhaust port, with each exhaust valve in a fully opened position so that it will be coated. If, at any time, the engine to be treated is equipped with exhaust collector rings that are difficult to remove, the exhaust valve must be sprayed through the spark plug hole instead of the exhaust port. This must be done with the exhaust valve fully opened and after the inside of the cylinder has been coated as outlined above.

(3) MAGNETOS. Magnetos shall be treated by lightly coating the steel parts with COMPOUND, rust-preventive, or with petrolatum.

(4) OPENINGS. All fuel and oil lines or open connections, cylinder ports and other openings shall be closed with suitable plugs, covers, etc. Threaded openings shall be closed with threaded plugs whenever practical. If wooden or similar tapered plugs are used, they shall be so constructed that they cannot be accidentally pushed or driven completely into the opening. When necessary, the rear oil tank vent connection plug shall be removed to prevent excess oil in the rear section from draining into the magneto while the engine is standing with the crankshaft in the vertical position. When this plug is removed, it will be wired to the engine as close as possible to the hole from which it was removed.

(5) SPARK PLUGS. Spark plugs will be removed, the spark plug holes will be oiled and then stopped by inserting shipping plugs, unserviceable spark plugs, corks, or wooden plugs. The removed plugs shall be cleaned, adjusted and tested; if serviceable, the spark plugs shall be coated with corrosion-preventive compound and placed in stock.

(6) EXTERIOR OF ENGINE. The exterior of the engine will be thoroughly cleaned with SOLVENT, dry-cleaning. A coating of COMPOUND, rust-preventive, will be applied on all unpainted steel parts.

SHIPMENT AND STORAGE

Rust appearing on any part before storage will be removed with sandpaper or a wire brush and the metal coated with corrosion-preventive compound, unless the surface was originally painted. Painted surfaces will be repainted.

(7) GASOLINE. Drain gasoline and return it to proper storage.

(8) BATTERIES. Remove the batteries from the vehicle. After plugging the vents in the cells, the case shall be cleaned with a solution of soda ash and water (8 ounces to the gallon) to neutralize the acid. After this treatment, the case will be flushed with cold water; do not use hot water or steam. Remove plugs from the vents after cleaning. Terminals and cable ends will be thoroughly cleaned with soda ash solution, scraping them clean with suitable tool or wire brush, and will then be greased with petrolatum or light grease. Hydrometer readings of cells will be taken and the battery charged, if readings are 1225 or less. Distilled water will be added to cover the plates, but not in excess of one quarter ($\frac{1}{4}$) inch above plates. Place the battery in active stock. Never allow batteries in stock to become discharged below a hydrometer reading of 1225; this will be a proper precaution against freezing in all but the most severe weather, when a specific gravity of 1250 shall be maintained.

(9) VEHICLE GENERAL. Rust appearing on any part before storage will be removed with sandpaper. Painted surfaces will be repainted and unpainted surfaces will be lightly coated with COMPOUND, rust-preventive.

(10) INSPECTION TAG. Attach a tag to the dash board. The dates of inspections will be entered on this tag and each initialed by the inspector.

f. Periodic Treatment of Vehicles in Dead Storage. At the expiration of each 3 month period, corrision-preventive treatment will be repeated, giving particular attention to the cylinders, valve compartments, and other internal parts. Under unfavorable climatic conditions, such as might occur in tropical climates or near salt water, it will be necessary to perform more frequent inspections and corrosion-preventive treatments in order to prevent damage to the equipment.

g. Check-up of Vehicles in Dead Storage. Vehicles will be inspected frequently to see that equipment or parts are not removed without proper authority.

h. Removing Vehicles from Dead Storage.

(1) MAGNETOS. Wipe the magnetos with a clean, dry rag to remove excess corrosion-preventive compound used and assemble magneto to the engine.

(2) CYLINDERS. Remove plugs from spark plug holes and pump out excess corrosion-preventive compound above the pistons with hand pump;

or if pump is not available, turn the engine over by hand to force out the corrosion-preventive compound.

(3) VALVES. Rotate the crankshaft through three or four revolutions by hand and observe for proper operation of valve mechanism. Any valve found to be sticking shall have the stem generously lubricated with penetrating oil or with a 50-50 mixture of kerosene and light lubricating oil. Continue to turn the engine over by hand until all evidence of sticking valves has been eliminated. If this treatment does not free the valves, necessary mechanical repairs to free them must be made before the engine is placed in service.

(4) GASOLINE TANK. Tank should be filled.

(5) SPARK PLUGS. New spark plugs should be installed in the engine.

(6) BATTERIES. Install fully charged batteries.

(7) TRANSMISSION, TRANSFER CASES, DIFFERENTIALS, AXLE HOUSING, ETC. Drain old lubricant from these units and other enclosed gears, flush thoroughly with OIL, lubricating, engine, SAE 10, and fill them to proper levels with the correct lubricant, using the lubrication section as a guide.

(8) ENGINE OIL TANK. Install the engine; fill the oil tank about half full. Since the material used as a corrosion-preventive on the interior surfaces of the engine mixes freely with engine oil, it will not be necessary to remove it prior to adding lubricating oil. Run the engine two or three hours, then drain the oil tank and add new oil to the system.

(9) LUBRICATION. The vehicle should be thoroughly lubricated before being placed in service.

(10) INSPECTION. A thorough inspection of the vehicle will be made upon the removal from dead storage. Any repairs that have been ordered on the inspection tag attached when the vehicle entered storage and which have not been previously made, must be taken care of at this time.

(11) STARTING ENGINE. Engine will be started according to the instructions given in section II, paragraph 9. Particular attention should be given to watching for overheating of the engine, excessive vibration, or any unusual noises that may indicate something is wrong.

92. STORAGE OF COMPONENTS AND EQUIPMENT.

a. Components removed from vehicles prior to storage must be thoroughly inspected and overhauled, if necessary, before being stored for reissue. These components, including engines, need not be retained in storage for any particular vehicle, but should be considered as stock when issue becomes necessary.

Section XXIII

REFERENCES

	Paragraph
Standard nomenclature lists	93
Explanatory publications	94

93. STANDARD NOMENCLATURE LISTS.

  a. Ammunition.

    Ammunition, revolver, automatic pistol, and submachine gun .... SNL T-2

    Ammunition, rifle, carbine, and automatic gun .. SNL T-1

    Firing tables and trajectory charts (index) .... SNL F-69

    Grenades, hand and rifle, and fuzing components. SNL S-4

  b. Armament.

    Gun, machine, cal. .30, Browning, M1919A4, fixed and flexible, and M1919A5, fixed, and ground mounts .... SNL A-6

    Gun, machine, cal. .50, Browning, heavy barrel, fixed and flexible, and ground mounts .... SNL A-39

    Gun, submachine, cal. .45, Thompson, M1928A1, and M1 .... SNL A-32

    Gun, 37-mm, M6 (tank) .... SNL A-45

  c. Maintenance.

    Cleaning, preserving and lubricating materials, recoil fluids, special oils, and miscellaneous related items .... SNL K-1

    Soldering, brazing and welding material, gases and related items .... SNL K-2

    Tools, maintenance, for repair of automatic guns, automatic gun antiaircraft materiel, automatic and semiautomatic cannon, and mortars ...... SNL A-35

  d. Tanks, heavy, M6 and M6A1 .... SNL G-118, Vols. I and II

  Current Standard Nomenclature Lists are as tabulated here. An up-to-date list of SNL's is maintained as the "Ordnance Publications for Supply Index" .... OPSI

94. EXPLANATORY PUBLICATIONS.

  a. Ammunition.

    Ammunition, general .... TM 9-1900

    Grenades .... FM 23-30

Qualifications in arms and ammunition training
allowances .... AR 775-10
Small-arms ammunition .... TM 9-1990

b. **Armament.**
Browning machine gun, cal. .30, HB, M2 (mounted
in combat vehicles)........................ FM 23-50
Browning machine gun, cal. .50, HB, M2 (mounted
in combat vehicles)........................ FM 23-65
Grenades .... FM 23-30
Thompson submachine gun, cal. .45, M1928A1.. FM 23-40

c. **Communications.**
Interphone equipment, RC-39................. TM 11-550
Radio fundamentals .... TM 11-455
Radio set, SCR 506.......................... TM 11-630
The radio operator .... TM 11-454

d. **Maintenance.**
Automotive brakes .... TM 10-565
Automotive electricity .... TM 10-580
Automotive lubrication .... TM 10-540
Automotive power transmission units......... TM 10-585
Chassis, body and trailer units............. TM 10-560
Cleaning, preserving, lubricating, and welding materials and similar items issued by the Ordnance
Department .... TM 9-850
Defense against chemical attack............. FM 21-40
Detailed lubrication instructions for ordnance materiel .... OFSB 6-series
Echelon system of maintenance............... TM 10-525
Fire prevention, safety precautions, accidents... TM 10-360
Motor transport inspections................. TM 10-545
Sheet metal work, body, fender and radiator repairs .... TM 10-450
The motor vehicle........................... TM 10-510
Tune-up and adjustment...................... TM 10-530

e. **Miscellaneous.**
Camouflage .... FM 5-20
Electric fundamentals .... TM 1-455
Fuels and carburetion....................... TM 10-550
List of publications for training, including training
films and film strips..................... FM 21-6
Military motor transportation............... TM 10-505
Military motor vehicles..................... AR 850-15

REFERENCES

Motor transport .... FM 25-10
The internal combustion engine .... TM 10-570

f. Storage and Shipment.

Rules governing the loading of mechanized and motorized Army equipment, also, major caliber guns for the United States Army and Navy, on open top equipment—published by the Operations and Maintenance Department of the Association of American Railroads

Storage of military motor vehicles .... AR 850-18

TM 9-721   HEAVY TANKS M6 AND M6A1
INDEX

A

	Page No.
Accelerator and hand throttle	13

Access to:
- accumulator sump tank 112
- engine 3
- expansion tank 110
- valve for filling and draining fluid circuit of converter 111

Accessories
- carried in vehicle
  - cal. .30 machine gun 52–53
  - cal. .45 submachine gun 53
  - 37-mm gun 53
  - 3-inch gun M7 53–54
- cold weather 62
- engine 81
- general discussion of 76
- inspection of 42
- miscellaneous 57–58

(See also Engine (and accessories))

"Accessory-end" of engine 77
Accumulator sump tank 112

Adjusting:
- carburetor 43
- sight on target 27
- steering and parking brakes ... 116
- track 8, 122–125
- voltage regulator 137

Air cleaners
- carburetor 84
- changing oil in 17
- 100-hour inspection 40

Air connections, maintenance 84
Ammeter 139

Ammunition
- boxes and racks, maintenance ... 68
- carried 9, 51
  - accessories 52–54
- cleaning exposed to vesicant gas .. 66
- stowage 27–28

Antiaircraft gun mount 26

Armament
- ammunition stowage 27–28
- carried in vehicle 51
- data on 9
- guns and gun mounts
  - antiaircraft gun mount 26
  - bow cal. .30 machine gun 26
  - combination mount T-49 ... 25–26
  - submachine guns 26
  - twin mount T-52 26

	Page No.
vision devices	27

Armor
- description 8
- turret 9

Assignment record, destroying before entering combat zone 52
Automatic shut-off valve 112–113
Automotive materiel, special precautions for 66
Auxiliary fluid pump (converter) .. 110

Auxiliary generating unit
- description 133–135
- location and use of 133
- operation 135

Auxiliary idler
- description 126
- removal and installation ... 126–127

Auxiliary steering mechanism, maintenance 70

B

Backfiring, cause and remedy 87
"Banjo" support beam 81

Batteries
- description 129
- maintenance 129–133
- storage treatment of 152
- unit to charge 9

Bayonet gage, use of 46–48
Blackout lights 141
Blocking vehicle for shipment 148

Bogie assembly
- description 8, 118
- inspection during engine warm-up. 21
- installation of 121–122
- maintenance 70
- operation and lubrication 118
- removal 118–121

Bogie wheels, inspection during engine warm-up 21
Booster, trouble shooting 142
Bow cal. .30 machine gun 26
Brackets and levers, maintenance .. 68
Brakes 13

(See also Hycon system)

C

Camouflage, paint as 147
Cap screws, inspection 41
Capacity of battery 129–133
Carbon dioxide, principle of ... 74–75

158

INDEX

C—Cont'd

	Page No.
Carburetor	
adjusting	43
install	99
leakage, cause	85
remove	94–95
Carburetor air cleaner	84
Carburetor air screen, 100-hour inspection	41
Carburetor fuel strainer, 100-hour inspection	41
Carburetor screen, cleaning	17
Care (and preservation)	
batteries	129
fire extinguisher	75
lubrication system	48
tools and equipment	60, 71
vehicles	50
Characteristics of vehicles	3
Chemicals, materiel affected by automotive materiel, special	
precautions for	66
decontamination	64–66
general discussion of	64
protective measures	64
Cleaning	
ammunition exposed to vesicant gas	66
carburetor screen	17
converter orifice vent valve	20
oil filter, edge-type	48
oil filters	16
oil pump finger strainer	17
vehicle	50
Clock	139
Clutch	14
Cold weather	
operating vehicle in	61–62
starting auxiliary generating unit	135
Combination mount T-49	25–26
Communication, data on	10
Company tools and equipment	71
Compartment, engine	3
Compass	14
Compression of cylinder, checking	42
Connecting rod assembly	80
Control linkages, checking	43
"Controlled differential"	116
Controls	
accelerator and hand throttle	13
brackets and levers, maintenance	68

	Page No.
brakes	13
cal. .30 bow machine gun elevation control lever	14
compass	14
driver, position of	11
fire detector light	16
fire extinguisher handles	16
fuel shut-off valve handles	16
gear shifting	14
illustration	12
instrument panel	14
oil pressure warning light	14–16
primer pump	14
siren control	14
steering controls	11–13
Converter, torque (See Torque converter)	
Converter fluid temperature gage	139
Converter oil cooler, 100-hour check	42
Converter oil pressure and temperature, 100-hour inspection	40
Converter oil pressure gage	139
Cooling operating fluid of torque converter	110
Cooling system	106
Corrosion-preventive treatment of vehicle for shipment	149
Crankcase, description	77
Crankcase breather screen, inspection	41
Crankshaft	
description	77–80
rotation of	77
Crew tools and equipment	71
Cylinder fins, inspection	41
Cylinders	
checking compression of	42
checking for oil or fuel in lower	17–18
description	77
firing order of	77
storage treatment of	150–151, 152–153
temperatures	
data	81
gage	139
100-hour inspection	40
Cylinders, work	113

D

	Page No.
Daily report (trip ticket) of inspection	32

D—Cont'd

	Page No.
Dash light switch	139

Data
- ammunition carried ... 9
- armament ... 9
- communication ... 10
- engine ... 9, 81–82
- fuel tanks ... 10
- general ... 9
- torque converter ... 111

Dead storage (*See* dead *under* Storage).

Decontamination of materiel ... 64–66

Definitions of echelons and maintenance terms ... 67

Description
- cooling system ... 106
- electrical system
  - auxiliary generating unit ... 133–135
  - batteries ... 129
  - lights ... 140–141
  - voltage regulator ... 135–136
- engine, Wright Cyclone ... 77
  (*See* description *under* Engine (and accessories) *for detailed information on components*)
- fire extinguishing system ... 71–73
- fuel system ... 101
- Hycon system ... 112–113
- power train ... 116
- suspension and tracks
  - auxiliary idler ... 126
  - bogie assembly ... 118
  - general ... 118
  - track supporting rollers ... 127
  - tracks ... 122
- torque converter ... 107–111
- vehicle ... 3–9

Desert operation of vehicle ... 63

Dielectric parts of magnetos, treating against moisture absorption ... 85

Differences in models ... 9

Differential, description ... 116–117

Dimensions of vehicle ... 9

Draining, transmission and final drive ... 117

Driver, position of ... 11

Driving sprockets ... 3–7

Driving vehicle
- controls, illustration ... 12
- precautions in ... 23–24
  (*See also* Operation and controls)

E

	Page No.
Echelons, definition of	67

Electric system
- auxiliary generating unit ... 133–135
- batteries ... 129–133
- fuse box ... 137
- instrument panel ... 138–141
- instruments, maintenance ... 141
- lights ... 140–141
- maintenance ... 68
- trouble shooting ... 141–144
- voltage regulator ... 135–137
  (*See under* above *names for detailed information*)

Engine (and accessories)
- data
  - fuel and lubrication system ... 82
  - general ... 9, 81
  - ignition ... 82
  - valves and timing ... 82
- description
  - accessories ... 81
  - crankcase ... 77
  - crankshaft ... 77–80
  - cylinders ... 77
  - engine supports ... 81
  - general ... 77
  - master and connecting rods ... 80
  - nomenclature, use of ... 77
  - pistons ... 80
  - valve operating mechanism ... 81
- install ... 96–100
  - components ... 98–99
  - 100-hour check ... 43
- lubrication system ... 44
- maintenance ... 68–69
- 100-hour inspection ... 40–42
- operation
  - precautions in ... 20
  - starting and warm-up ... 18–20
  - inspection during ... 20–21
  - stopping ... 23
- periodic inspection
  - 50-hour ... 82
  - 100-hour ... 83
- removal ... 91–96
  - components interfering with ... 92–95
- starting in cold weather ... 62
- storage treatment of ... 150, 151–152

INDEX

E—Cont'd   Page No.

Engine (and accessories)—Cont'd
  trouble shooting
    carburetor air cleaner 84
    carburetor leakage 85
    engine fails to start 83–84
    engine runs but does not stop .. 84
    engine starts, but stops 84
    general discussion of 83
    localizing and reporting
      troubles 82–83
    low power and uneven running . 84
    procedure 86–91
    spark plugs and magnetos 85
  type 3

Engine compartment
  function of 3
  100-hour check 43
  shrouds
    install and connect 98
    remove 95
  top plate and guard
    install 99
    remove 91–92

Engine gasoline, grades of 105
Engine oil cooler, 100-hour check ... 42
Engine oil pressure and temperature,
  100-hour inspection 39
Engine oil pressure gage 139
Engine oil temperature gage 139
Engine primer pump 14
Engine support beam
  connect 98
  disconnect 96

Engine support brackets
  connect 97–98
  disconnect 96
Engine supports 81
Equipment
  miscellaneous, carried on
    vehicles 57–58
  signaling 58–59
  (See also Tools (and equipment))
Exhaust system, 100-hour inspection. 42
Expansion tank
  checking converter oil level 20
  checking operating fluid
    level in 17
  description and functions 110
Extinguishing system, fire, maintenance 69

F

Failure to start engine 83–84
  cause and remedy 86–87

                       Page No.

"Fast" fires 74
50-hour inspection of
  engine 82
  vehicle 33–39
Filling transmission and final drive. 117
Filter elements of air cleaner,
  inspection 84
Filters for reduction gear oil and
  converter fluid 110
Final drive
  filling and draining 117
  lubrication of 116–117
  maintenance 70
  oil pressure and temperature,
    100-hour inspection 40
  oil pressure gage 139
  oil temperature gage 139
Finger strainer, oil pump,
  cleaning 17
Fire detector light 16
Fire extinguisher handles 16
Fire extinguishing system (See fire
  extinguishing system under Tools
  (and equipment))
Firing order of cylinders 77
Fluid, operating medium of
  torque converter 107–110
Fluid for torque converter 7
Fluid level in expansion tank,
  checking 17
Fuel, checking for in lower
  cylinders 17–18
Fuel gage 139
Fuel inlet line, main (See Main fuel
  inlet line)
Fuel leaks
  checking for 16
  100-hour inspection 40
Fuel lines
  description and function 101
  inspection 43
  storage treatment of 151
Fuel shut-off valves
  description and function 101
  handles 16
Fuel system
  data 82
  description 101
  grades of engine gasoline 105
  illustration 102
  inspection 104
  maintenance 69
  trouble shooting 104

TM 9-721 HEAVY TANKS M6 AND M6A1

F—Cont'd

	Page No.
Fuel tanks, data on	10
Fuse box	137

G

Gas, materiel affected by (See Chemicals, materiel affected by)	
Gasoline, engine, grades of	105
Gasoline, fires involving	74
Gear shifting (See Shifting)	
Generator	
install	99
remove	93–94
Grades of:	
engine gasoline	105
oil, specifications	
lubrication system	82
transmission and final drive	117
Gravity, specific, of battery	129–133
Guide, lubrication	44
Gun, machine, cal. .30	
accessories	52–53
armament tools	57
spare parts	54–55
Gun, machine, cal. .50	
spare parts	55–56
Gun, 37-mm, M6	
accessories	53
spare parts	56
Gun, 3-inch, M7	
accessories	53–54
spare parts	56–57
Gun, submachine, cal. .45	
accessories	53
spare parts	55
Gun firing control lever	13
Gun safety switch	138
Guns and gun mounts (See guns and gun mounts under Armament)	

H

Hand grenades, stowage of	28
Hand throttle	13
Headlights	140–141
High oil consumption, cause and remedy	90–91
High temperature, operation of vehicle at	63
Hull (assembly)	
armor of (front section)	8
differences in construction	9
inspection of for oil leaks under maintenance	20–21, 70
Hycon pressure, 100-hour inspection	40
Hycon pressure gage	138

	Page No.
Hycon steering controls	11–13
Hycon system	
description	112–113
inspection and maintenance	113–114
trouble shooting	114–115
Hydraulic pump	
inspection	114
use of	112
Hydraulic steering and braking (See Hycon system)	
Hydraulic torque converter (See Torque converter)	

I

Idler(s)	
location and use	8
(See Auxiliary idler)	
Ignition, data on	82
Ignition harness, inspection	41
Ignition switch assembly	138
Inspection	
after operation	30–32
daily report (trip ticket)	32
first echelon report	31
at halt	29–30
cooling system	106
during engine warm-up	20–21
engine	
50-hour	82
100-hour	83
50-hour, vehicle	33–39
fuel system	104
Hycon system	114
lubrication system	48
100-hour	39–43
prestarting	16–18
purpose of	29
technical, of vehicle in storage	150
torque converter	111
tracks	21
vehicle removed from storage	153
voltage regulator	137
Instrument panel	
checking	18
illustration	15
list of instruments	138–140
location and use	14
Instruments, maintenance of	140
Instruments and panels, maintenance	69
Intake pipes, inspection	42

J

Jumper, use of	141

INDEX

L

	Page No.
Leak(s) (-age)	
carburetor, cause	85
checking for in Hycon system	114
oil and fuel	
checking for	16
100-hour inspection	40
"Left" side of engine	77
illustration	79
Lever, cal. .30 bow machine gun elevation control	14
Light switch	139
Lights	
blackout lights and tail lamps	141
fire detector	16
headlights	140–141
siren	141
Limited storage of vehicles	150
Linkages, control, checking	43
Loading vehicle for shipment	148–149
Localizing engine troubles	83
"Log Book," use of	50
Low power of engine	84
cause and remedy	87
Low pressure, Hycon pump, cause and remedy	115
Lower cylinders, checking for oil or fuel in	17–18
Lubrication	
bogie assembly	118
engine lubrication system	44
guide	44
inspections	48
reports and records	49
torque converter lubrication system	46–48
track supporting rollers	128
transmission and final drive	116–117
trouble shooting	48
Lubricating devices, painting	147
Lubrication system	
data on	82
maintenance	69
Lung irritant casualties	65

M

	Page No.
Magneto lubricating felt, inspection	41
Magneto sump plug, inspection	42
Magnetos	
storage treatment of	151, 152
trouble shooting	85, 142–143
when switching, cause and remedy	88
Main electrical switch	140

	Page No.
Main fuel inlet line	
connect	98
disconnect	96
Maintenance	
air connections	84
cooling system	106
duties of using arms personnel	
boxes, racks, ammunition	68
controls, brackets and levers	68
definition of echelons and terms	67–68
electrical system	68
engine	68–69
extinguishing system, fire	69
fuel system	69
hull assembly	69
instruments and panels	69
lubrication system	69
mechanism, auxiliary, steering	70
oil lines	69
suspension assembly, track	70
torque converter, transmission, and final drive units	70
turret assembly	70
vehicle assembly	70
Hycon system	113–114
instruments	140
preventive (See Inspection)	
scope of	67
tracks	122
Maintenance, protective, vehicle in cold weather	61–62
Manual steering controls	13
Manual steering lever, use	22
Marking equipment for shipment	148
Master and connecting rods, description	80
Materiel affected by chemicals (See Chemicals, materiel affected by)	
Mechanism, auxiliary, steering, maintenance	70
Metal surfaces, painting	146
Misfiring, cause and remedy	143
Models, differences in	9
Moisture absorption, treating dielectric parts of magnetos against	85
Motor Book, use of	50
Mounts, gun (See guns and gun mounts under Armament)	
Mufflers	
install	99
remove	92

	Page No.
N	
Nomenclature, use of for engine	77
Numbering of cylinders	77
Nuts, inspection	41
O	
Oil	
capacity and grade of for lubricating transmission and final drive	117
changing of in air cleaners	17
checking for in lower cylinders	17–18
consumption and grade of, data on	82
fires involving	74
lubrication of transmission and final drive	116–117
servicing carburetor air cleaner with	84
Oil consumption	
data on	82
high, cause and remedy	90–91
Oil cooler, converter, 100-hour check	42
Oil cooler, 100-hour check	42
Oil dilution switch	138–139
Oil dilution valve, operation	44
Oil filter, cleaning	16, 48
Oil inlet and oil outlet lines	
connect	98
disconnect	96
Oil leaks	
checking for	16
inspect for under hull	20–21
100-hour inspection	40, 41
Oil lines	
inspection	43
maintenance	70
storage treatment of	151
Oil pressure	
checking	48
loss of, cause and remedy	88–90
Oil pressure and temperature, 100-hour inspection	39
Oil pressure relief valve, inspection	48
Oil pressure warning light	14–16
Oil pump	
priming	43
testing operation of	48
Oil pump finger strainer, cleaning	17
Oil pump pressure line	
connect	98
disconnect	95–96
Oil sump	
draining	48

	Page No.
filling and description	46–48
Oil sump strainer, 100-hour inspection	41
Oil supply for torque converter, reduction gear lubrication system	46
Oil tank, filling	44
Oil temperature line	
connect	98
disconnect	96
Oilholes, cleaning	50
100-hour inspection	39–43
cooling system	106
engine	83
vehicle	39–43
Operating fluid, gages for	111
Operation (*See also* Operation and controls)	
auxiliary generating unit	135
engine (*See* operation *under* Engine)	
fire extinguishing system	73–74
inspection after	30–32
daily report (trip ticket)	32
first echelon report	31
inspection of Hycon	114
suspension and tracks	118
testing oil pumps	48
under unusual conditions	
cold weather	61–62
accessories	62
desert operation	63
high temperatures	63
Operation and controls	
Controls (*See* Controls)	
engine	
starting and warm-up	18–20
stopping	23
general discussion of	11
inspection	
during engine warm-up	20–21
prestarting	16–18
operating the vehicle	21–23
precautions	23–24
Organization maintenance (*See* Maintenance)	
Organization spare parts and accessories	76
Organization tools	71
Orifice valve, use of	110
Over-all dimension of vehicle	9
Overheated engine, cause and remedy	87–88

INDEX

P

	Page No.
Paint(-ing)	
as camouflage	146
general discussion of	145
lubricating devices	147
metal surfaces	146
preparing for	145–146
removing	146–147
Panel, instrument	14
illustration	15
(See also Instrument Panel)	
Parking brakes	
adjustment	116
description and use	13
Pedal	7
Performance of engine, indication of	22
Periodic inspection	
cooling system (100-hour)	106
engine	
50-hour	82
100-hour	83
Periscopes	27
Piston(s)	
description	80
displacement	77
Portable fire extinguishers	75
Power, transmission of through converter	107
Power, train	
description	116
steering and parking brakes, adjustment	116
transmission and final drive, lubrication of	116–117
Precautions	
lubrication system	48
operating vehicle	23–24
Pressure, low, in Hycon pump	115
Pressure control valve	113
Prestarting inspection	16–18
Preventive maintenance of vehicle in cold weather	61–62
(See also Inspection)	
Primer line	
connect	98
disconnect	95
Primer pump	14
Priming oil pump	43
Push rod hoses, checking	42

R

Ratchet of steering lever	13

TM 9-721

	Page No.
Rebuild, definition of	68
Records (See Reports and records)	
Reduction gear oil level, checking	17
Reduction gear oil pump and pump and sump	110
Regimental tools and equipment	71
Repair, definition of	68
Replace, definition of	67
Reports and records	
first echelon, mechanical inspection	31
lubrication servicing	49
tools and equipment	60, 71
vehicle	50
Reverse, placing vehicle in	22
"Right" side of engine	77
illustration	78
Rotation of crankshaft	77

S

	Page No.
Service, definition of	67
Service brakes	13
Servicing air cleaners	84
Shifting	
operation	7, 14
transmission brake	13
Shipment of vehicle	148–149
Shrouds (See shrouds under Engine compartment)	
Sighting equipment carried on vehicle	51–52
Siren	141
Siren control	14
"Slow" fires	74
Sockets	140
Spare parts	
gun, machine, cal. .30	54–55
gun, machine, cal. .50	55–56
gun, submachine, cal. .45	45–55
gun, 37-mm, M6	56
gun, 3-inch, M7	56–57
organization	76
Spark plugs	
inspection	41
storage treatment	151
trouble shooting	85, 142
Specific gravity of battery electrolyte	129–133
Speedometer	138
Sprockets, inspection of during engine warm-up	21
Starter solenoid, trouble shooting	142

TM 9-721   HEAVY TANKS M6 AND M6A1

S — Cont'd

	Page No.
Starting	
engine	18–20
failure	83–84, 86–87
in cold weather	62
inspection of vehicle before	18
Starting motor	
install	98–99
remove	92
Steering (See Hycon system)	
Steering brakes, adjustment of	116
Steering controls	11–13
Steering levers	13
Steering mechanism, auxiliary, maintenance	70
Steering the vehicle	22
Stop light switches	13
Stopping:	
engine	23
vehicle	22
Storage	
components and equipment	153
conditions	149
dead	
periodic treatment and check-up of vehicles in	152
placing vehicles in	150–152
removing vehicles from	152–153
instructions, general	149
limited	150
technical inspections	150
Stowage, ammunition	27–28
Submachine guns	26
Suction control valve	112
Sump, oil drawn from	46
Support rollers, inspection of during engine warm-up	21
Supports, engine	81
Suspension and tracks	
auxiliary idler	126–127
bogie assembly	118–122
description and operation	118
track supporting rollers	127–128
tracks	122–126
volute springs	122
(See under above names for detailed information)	
Suspension assembly, maintenance	70
Synchronization of sight and gun	27

T

	Page No.
Tachometer	138
Tachometer shaft	
connect	98
disconnect	96
Tail lamps	141
Telescopic sight	27
Temperature data, battery	129–133
Temperature ranges	61
Temperatures, 100-hour inspection of	39–40
Test light	141
Test run of vehicle after 100-hour check	43
Testing:	
oil pump operation	48
wire	141–142
Tools (and equipment)	
cal. .30 machine gun	57
fire extinguishing system	
carbon dioxide, principle of	74–75
care of	75
description	71–73
maintenance	69
operation	73–74
portable fire extinguishers	75
organization tools	71
pioneer	59
vehicular	59–60
Torque converter	
data on	111
inspection	111
location and description	3–7, 107–111
lubrication system	46–48
maintenance	70
100-hour check	43
Track supporting rollers	
description	127
lubrication	128
removal	127
Track(s)	
adjustment	122–125
description	7–8, 122
inspection during engine warm-up	21
installation	126
maintenance	122
removal	125–126
Transmission	
filling and draining	117
lubrication of	116–117
power train	116
Transmission assembly, maintenance	70
Transmission brake	13
Transmission oil pressure gage	139

INDEX

T—Cont'd

Trouble shooting
  electrical system
    booster 142
    general 143–144
    jumper 141
    magneto 142–143
    replacing defective wire ... 141–142
    spark plugs 142
    test light 141
    testing wire 141–142
    voltage regulator and starter solenoid 142
  engine (See trouble shooting under Engine (and accessories))
  fuel system 104
  Hycon system 114–115
  lubrication system 48
Turret, armor of 9
Turret assembly, maintenance 70
Twin mount T-52 26

U

Uneven running of engine 84, 87
Unusual conditions, operation under 61–63
Using arms personnel, duties of (See duties of using arms personnel under Maintenance)

V

Valve, orifice, use of 110
Valve clearance, checking 42
Valve operating mechanism 81
Valve(s)
  filling and draining fluid circuit of converter 110–111
  treatment of when vehicle is removed from storage 153
Valves and timing, data on 82
Vehicle
  armament 25–28
  care and preservation 50

chemicals, materiel affected by. 64–65
cooling system 106
data 9–10
description and characteristics ... 3–9
differences in models 9
electrical system 129–142
engine and accessories 77–100
fuel system 101–105
Hycon system 112–115
lubrication 44–49
maintenance 67–68, 70
operation and controls 11–24
organization spare parts and accessories 76
painting 145–147
power train 116–117
preventive maintenance (inspection) 29–43
removing engine from 98
shipment and storage 148–153
suspension and tracks 118–128
tools, accessories, and equipment carried in 51–60
tools and equipment 71–75
torque converter 107–111
Vehicular tools 59–60
Vesicant casualties 65
Vesicants, liquid, removal of 64–66
Vision devices 27
Voltage regulator
  description 135–136
  inspection and adjustment 137
  trouble shooting 142
Voltmeter 139
Volute springs, removal and installation 121

W

Warm-up and starting engine 18–20
  inspection during 20–21
Wire
  replacing defective 142
  testing 141–142
  use of test light for 141
Work cylinders 113

TM 9-721 **HEAVY TANKS M6 AND M6A1**

$$\begin{bmatrix} \text{A.G. 062.11 (2-5-43)} \\ \text{O.O. 461/33360 (2-5-43)} \end{bmatrix}$$

BY ORDER OF THE SECRETARY OF WAR:

OFFICIAL:
                               G. C. MARSHALL,
  J. A. ULIO,   *Chief of Staff.*
     Major General,
       The Adjutant General.

DISTRIBUTION:

  R 9(2); IR 17(2); Bn 9(1); IBn 17(5); C 9(4); IC 17(5)

(For explanation of symbols, see FM 21-6)

Also Now Available!

Visit us at:

www.PeriscopeFilm.com

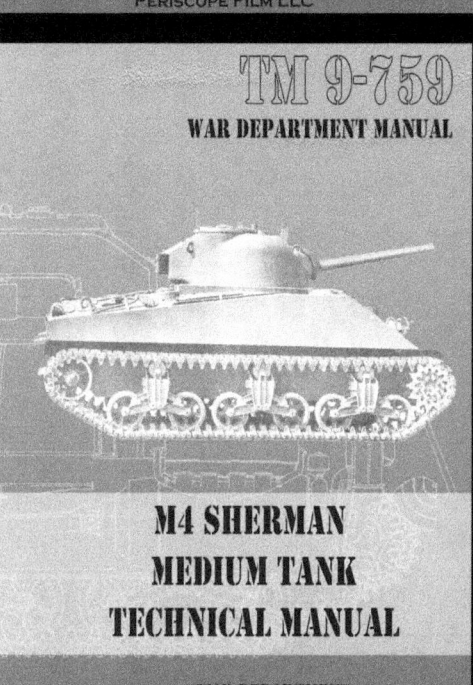
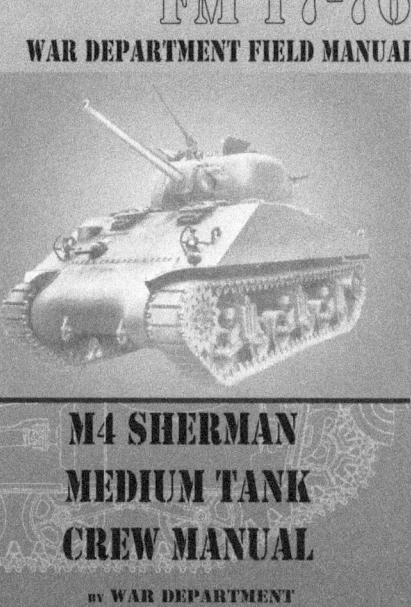

©2011 PERISCOPE FILM LLC
ALL RIGHTS RESERVED
ISBN #978-1-935700-83-8
WWW.PERISCOPEFILM.COM

www.ingramcontent.com/pod-product-compliance
Lightning Source LLC
LaVergne TN
LVHW051834080426
835512LV00018B/2866